A Nurturing Darkness

Meditations on the Root Cellars of Newfoundland

The Artwork of
Carol Bajen-Gahm

with a commentary by
Emily Deming

number two in the
Komatik Press
Artists' Series

Komatik Press
Cambridge, St. John's

Artists' Series

Published in Canada by

Komatik Press

62 Lower Street, Torbay,

Newfoundland and Labrador,

A1K 1B3

www.komatikpress.com

rexkomatik@gmail.com

www.bajengahm.com

ISBN (paperback) 978-1-950065-99-8

ISBN (hardcover) 978-1-950065-00-4

ISBN (eBook) 978-1-950065-01-1

Book design by

Rex Passion and Carol Bajen-Gahm

Cover design by Rex Passion

Komatik Press Artists' Series

Introduction

In 2019, we created the Komatik Press *Artists' Series* to celebrate the visual artists of Newfoundland and Labrador, to explore the amazing diversity of their artistic practices, and to give artists an opportunity to talk about their work in their own words.

We are an experimental publisher using digital printing technology to discover areas that would not be open to traditional publishers due to cost. We use digital design, on-demand printing and distribution, and social media to reach a worldwide readership at a reasonable price with both print and e-books. We want to use this revolutionary technology to expose a large audience to a wide diversity of art and artists. We plan to examine a broad range of artistic forms: painting, sculpture, fiber art, photography, furniture, jewellery, street art and others; from many different groups of artists. For us at Komatik Press, this will be an exciting journey and we hope it will contribute to a wider appreciation for the grand diversity of art and artists in Newfoundland and Labrador. I am sure there will be some unexpected twists along the way.

Rex Passion
Komatik Press
Torbay, Newfoundland
2020

The Nurturing Darkness: Meditations on the Root Cellars of Newfoundland

The Artwork of Carol Bajen-Gahm

Carol Bajen-Gahm is a mixed media artist with her studio on a cliff overlooking Torbay Bight only a few kilometers from St. John's, Newfoundland. In frequent storms, the sea tosses pebbles against the building; icebergs, whales, sea birds, huge waves and shoals of capelin are common visitors. An ever-changing creek flows into the ocean, or not. Carol and her studio are literally immersed in the wild surroundings of the North Atlantic and, as a consequence, her art is steeped in the soul of Newfoundland.

With encaustic and oil paints, seaweed prints, netting, photo transfers and other media, Carol distills the essence of root cellars. Many are still extant in Newfoundland outports and still preserving food during the cold winter months.

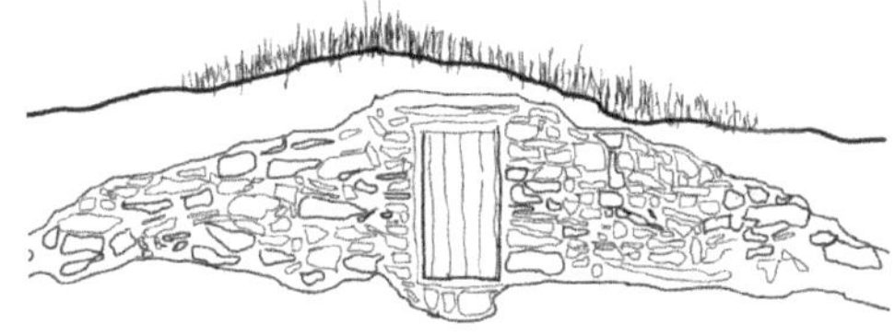

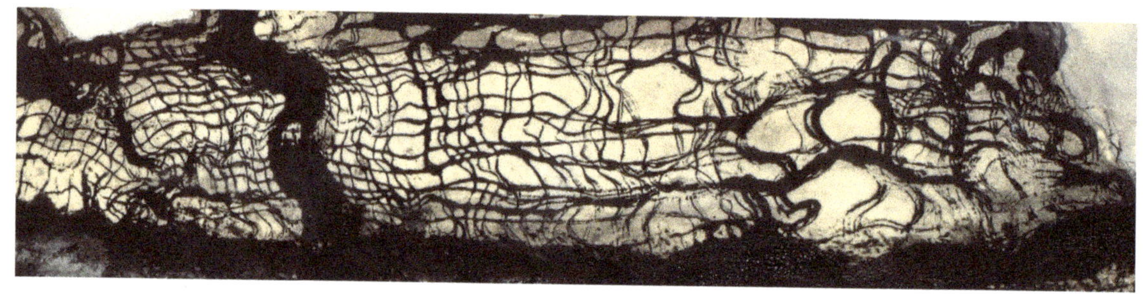

Artist's Statement 2020

My grandfather, a Presbyterian missionary, impressed on me the importance of living a life of service. He believed that the disciplines of art and music were inflated and frivolous life paths. This never made sense to me; in fact, I believed quite the opposite.

Art and music nurture the human soul, and it is as important to feed the spirit as it is to feed the body. Much work is being done in this area, and there is now evidence to support the theory that the interface between the two resides in the immune system, and it is clear to me that a healthy psyche is essential to overall wellness. The rampant rise of auto-immune diseases points to a world starved for vital images.

The observation that the opposite of aesthetic is anesthetic startled me into realizing the importance of being alive to the senses, alive to beauty, rather than succumbing to numbness.

My aim is to create works of deep nourishing beauty, not the kind of beauty that floats on the surface, but a kind with a shadow; one that has been informed by darkness; beauty that is abstract, spiritual, meditative and healing.

Dark, confined spaces, like the interiors of root cellars, have always attracted me. They are often the settings of fairy tales and dreams and engender fear which, with work, can lead to deeper understanding and become a soul-nurturing force.

Carol Bajen-Gahm
Torbay, Newfoundland
2020

Carol Bajen-Gahm's Root Cellar Meditations

by

Emily Deming

This series by Carol Bajen-Gahm is with me as I shovel snow. The physical work of it. The layers. Chipping away at some, sluffing off more. Going in hard to be met with ease, then relaxing only to come up on ice or rock. Shades of white yellow grey black gravel water rock salt.

Bajen-Gahm says, "when I first started, I second-guessed myself. I wouldn't let anyone go into the studio. I was afraid to tell people how I work... now... it's how I work."

The front path is almost cleared and I'm sweating from labour and from being watched. I'm figuring my way through this frozen slush in front of strangers hiding behind their parlour curtains. Am I supposed to pile it there? How do they hold the

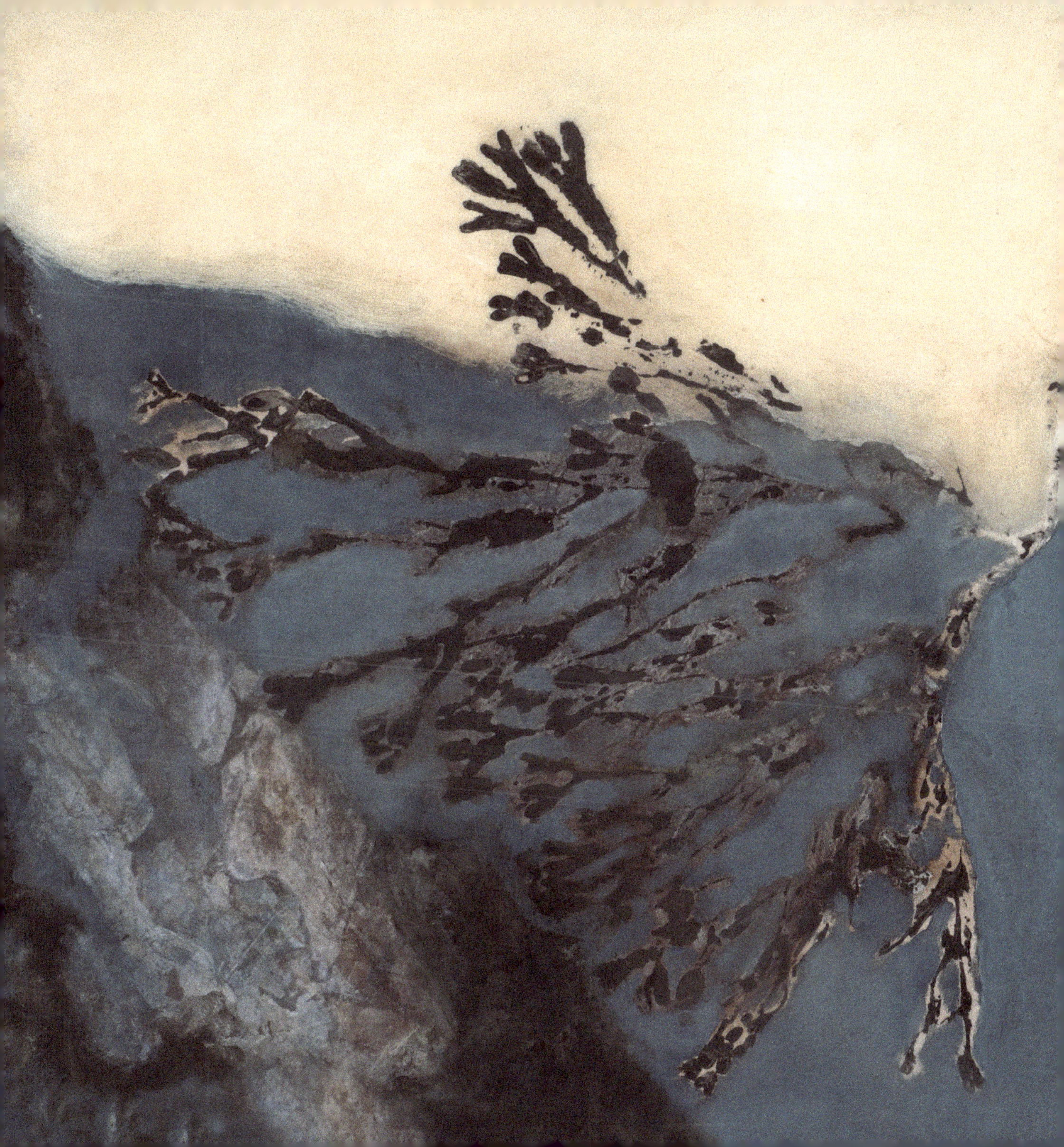

metal shovel? How did their fathers hold it? Should I apologize? Is this how it's done? Are they watching from across the street when I stop and crouch and stare at the intricate crenulations of one snowfall layered with exhaust then buried by the next, then sliced by plow and shovel? Accumulations of nature's detritus in remote manmade corners.

The corner of three planes meeting, forms the entrance into Bajen-Gahm's *Root Cellar Meditations*. But the way in is less direct. The careful balance of the elements in each piece refuses to direct us where to begin. The doorways become objects; the objects are paths to unseen worlds. She admits she intentionally obscures perspective with an "element of trying to be evocative." Are you looking at something, or is that "something," something else?

The work she has done to balance the pieces we must match by unbalancing our point of view. We may draw ourselves in by moving towards and into, then away and above. Each piece, and even each detail within each piece, reveals a different path to different worlds depending on a macro vs a micro view; an aerial vs a frontal perspective. Like every true fairytale, choice is as powerful as fate.

Also like fairy tales, these pieces are about place. Place through colour and shape. Place "funnelled through the subconscious" and abstracted by the artist. The sense of depth and of danger is very real, and the colours she pulls from everywhere around her. The Atlantic Ocean, right below her studio in Torbay, Newfoundland is "so multicoloured with the atmosphere and with what is growing under it; it can look Caribbean, even though you know…" What she knows, what we know from the work, is the danger of the deep, the scarcity of warmth, and hence its value. Root cellars must not freeze; must not overheat. Small dark pockets of stable temperature and still air, pockmarking a coast of ice and wind and violent mutability.

"Living above a rock beach you can watch changes dramatically - one day the fresh water is flowing under the rocks into the ocean, the next day it breaks through. Large yellow rocks once known, were covered and did not reappear until years later. Large forces change the beach; The beach changes with each wave."

The colours in these works "bloom mysteriously out of the dark." Each series she does brings out a certain element of colour, though Bajen-Gahm "tr[ies] not to be seduced by it." She uses "tertiary colours" (where at least three colours are mixed to form the right one.) The R&F encaustics (a wax based paint) that she uses have up to seven pigments in each colour. Bajen-Gahm, who also teaches workshops out of her studio, says students "shiver in their boots" the day they learn that.

For the *Root Cellar Meditations* she used Sumi ink to add prints of damp seaweed and netting on the Rives paper. She could then cover that image and then scrape back through the encaustics and it would still be there. She also used charcoal and graphite for different blacks. Cold wax doesn't change the quality of black, hot wax covers the black then you can scrape back through to it. She was pushing for how many different kinds of black she could get. With those blacks are browns decaying to gold; blues so dense they must be generating their own light as none could penetrate through the ferocity of the colour; rusts that are almost an action, a growth, a puddle, proof of happening.

But it is those blacks that unite and distinguish this series from the artist's previous works. She, "wanted to always have a dark element." Though which element that is shifts with each piece. These are mixed media, not collage, but she "sure as hell mix[es] the media," with photo transfer elements and the prints from ocean jetsam. There are "ghost prints" made with a second pressing after only a residue of the ink remained. Bajen-Gahm learned to leave such details. "Restraint," she says "was a huge part of this series." While some parts she "struggled to bring into balance, [...] others had something precious to preserve."

These works show skills of intuition accumulated from constant experimentation. Skill so solid at this point in her career she can become a sort of medium for her own work. A medium is a conduit, but the nature of a given medium affects the substance flowing through it. Bajen-Gahm explains, "you have to let the painting be itself. It speaks. It's not you controlling it. I may have had other ideas. The painting demanded what happened. [...] You start it. Bring balance and colour and - boom! - like a novelist, you go to kill off a character and the damn character won't go. You have to give in. You can't enforce your will on a painting. People do. But you can't."

Bajen-Gahm may not be able to control them, but she is the

only one who could create them. Now, unleashed, they continue their lichen-like growth in us, the viewers. They enter our minds and alter us as our viewing alters them. I see these works in variations all around me: in snow, in safe havens and rough weather, in fine lines, in cracks, in grief and anticipation, in burnt hair on raku pottery and in heavy echoes of old tales. Having seen this series, the world is forever a deeper, more penetrable mystery.

Root Cellar # 1
24" x 20" (61 x 50.8 cm)
2017

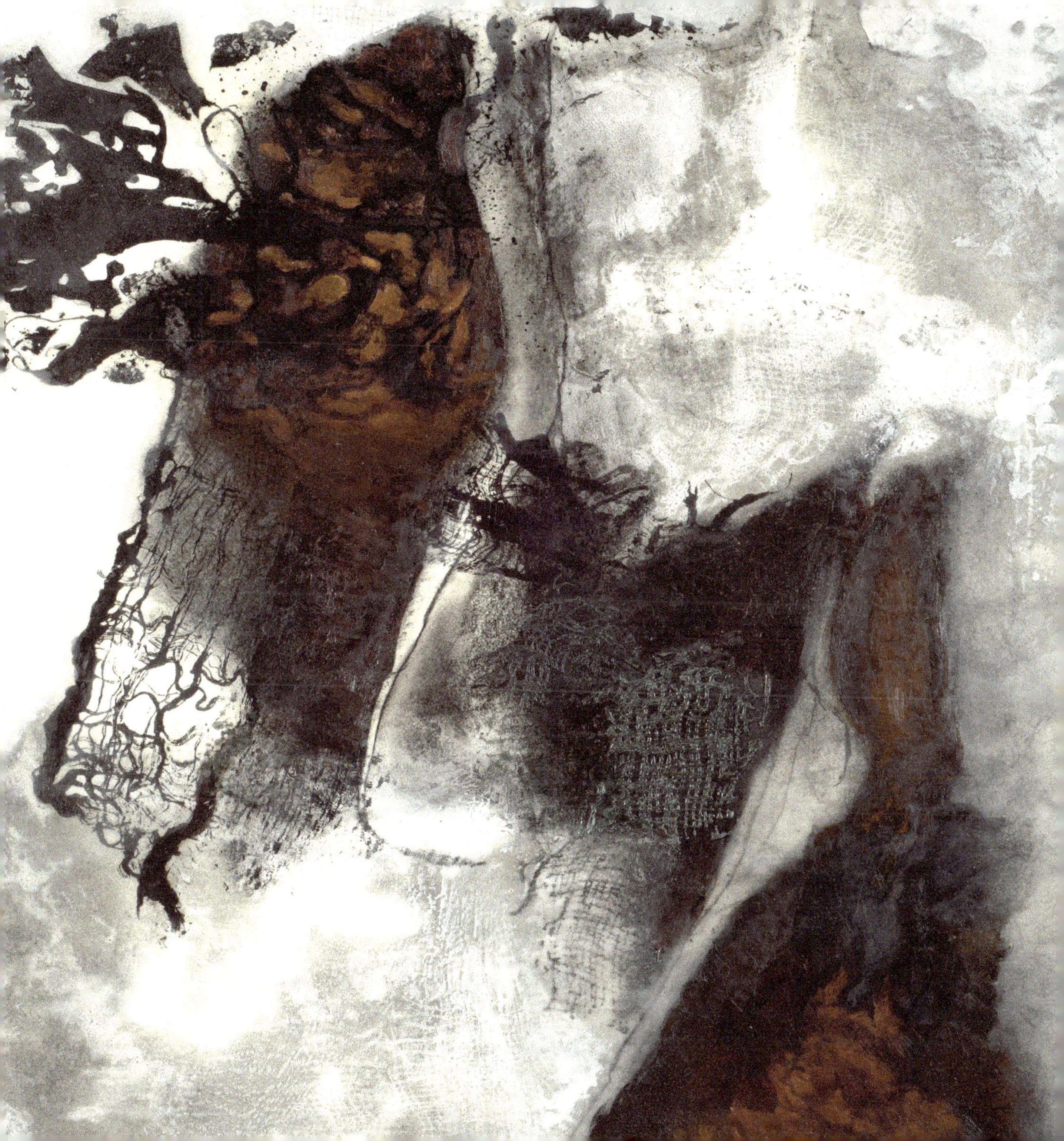

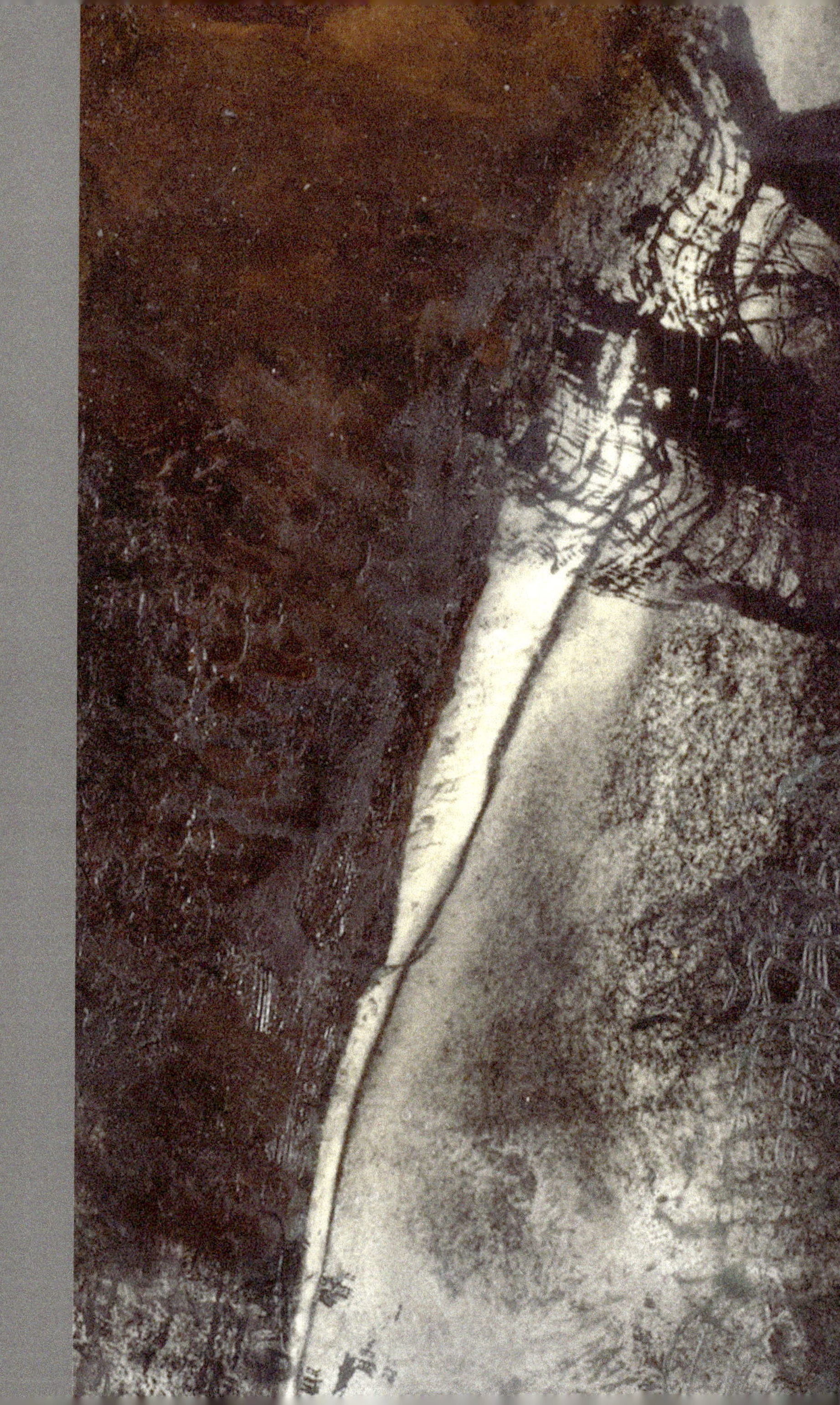

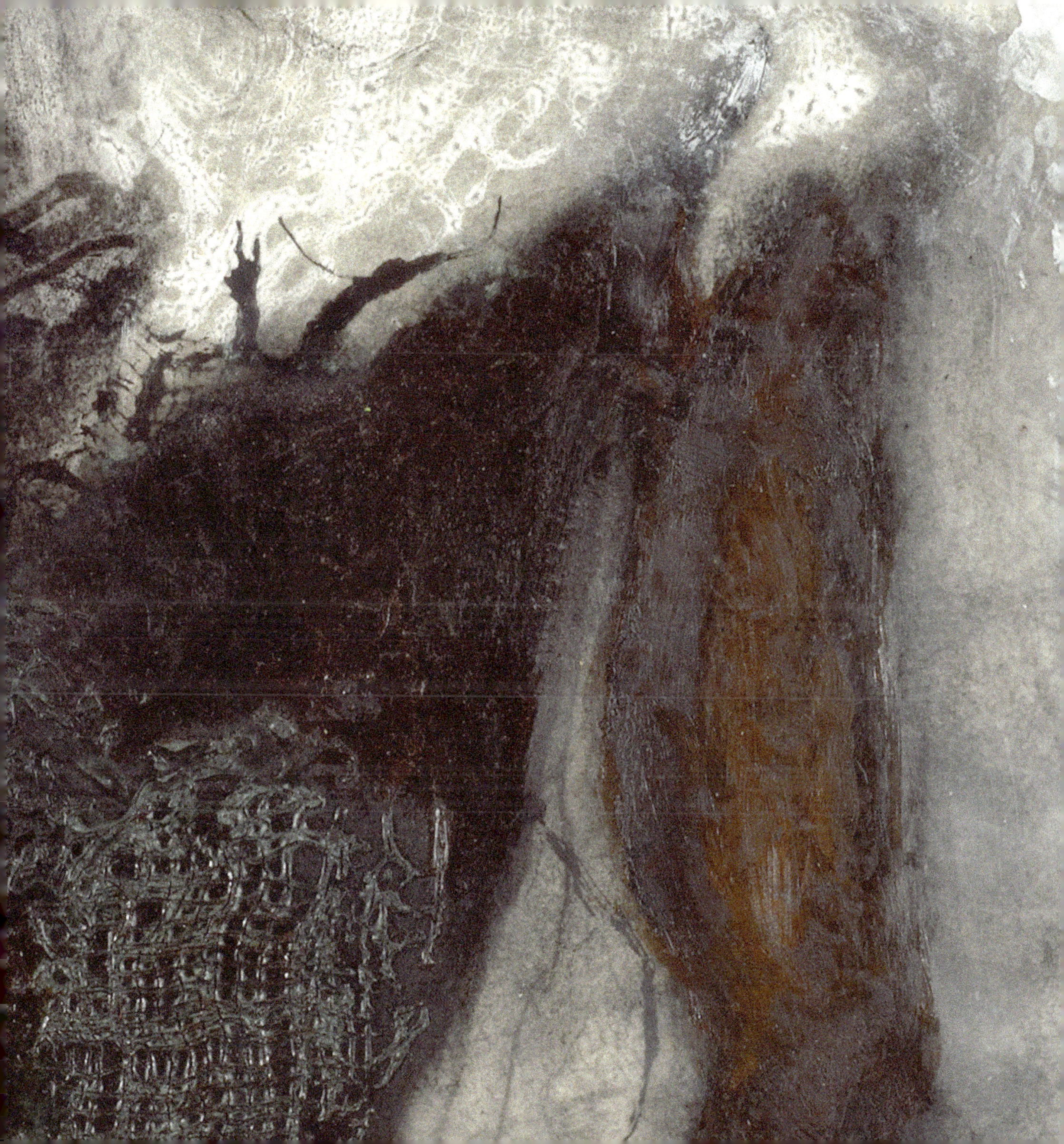

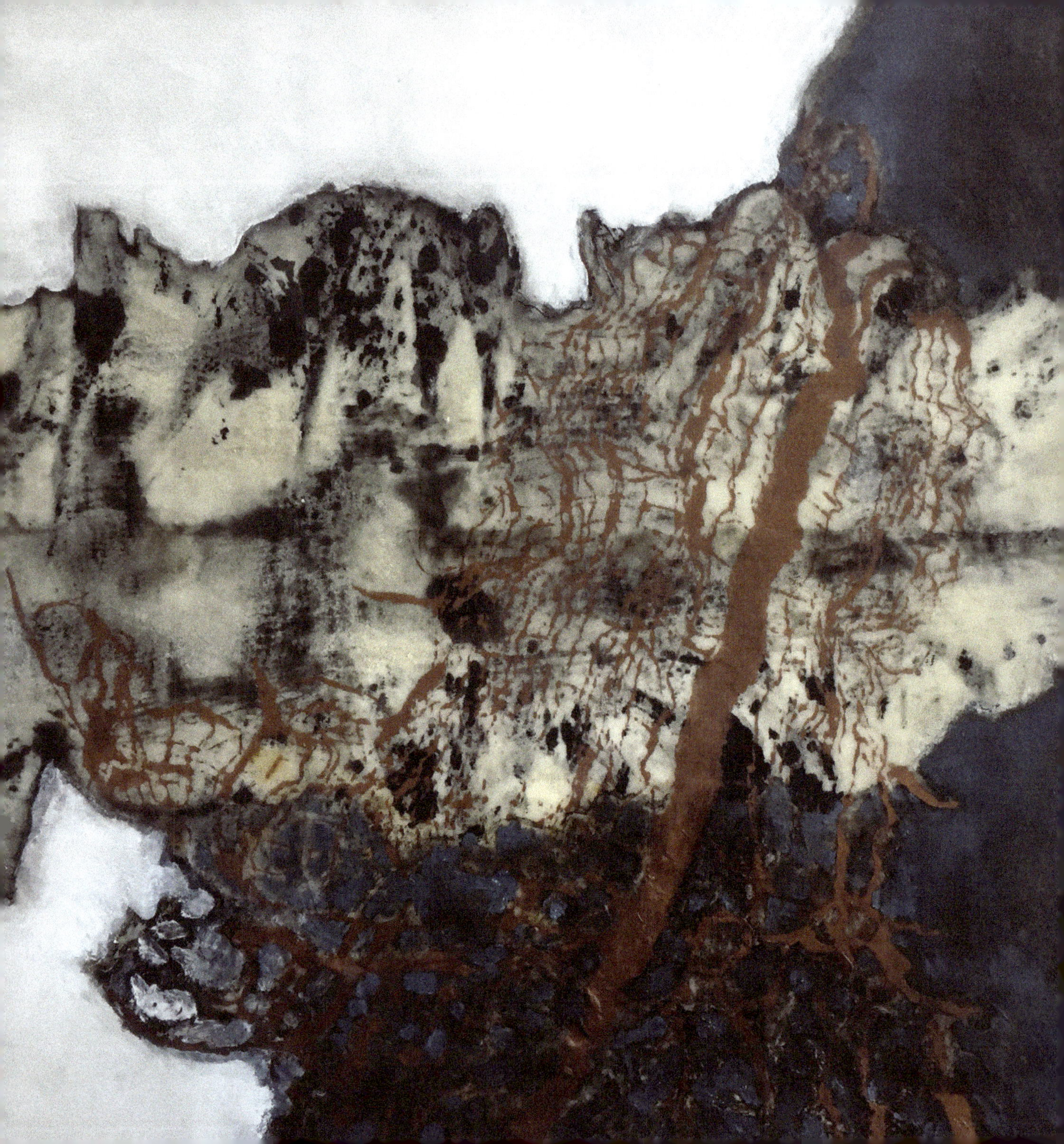

Root Cellar # 22
12" x 12" (30.5 x 30.5 cm)
2017

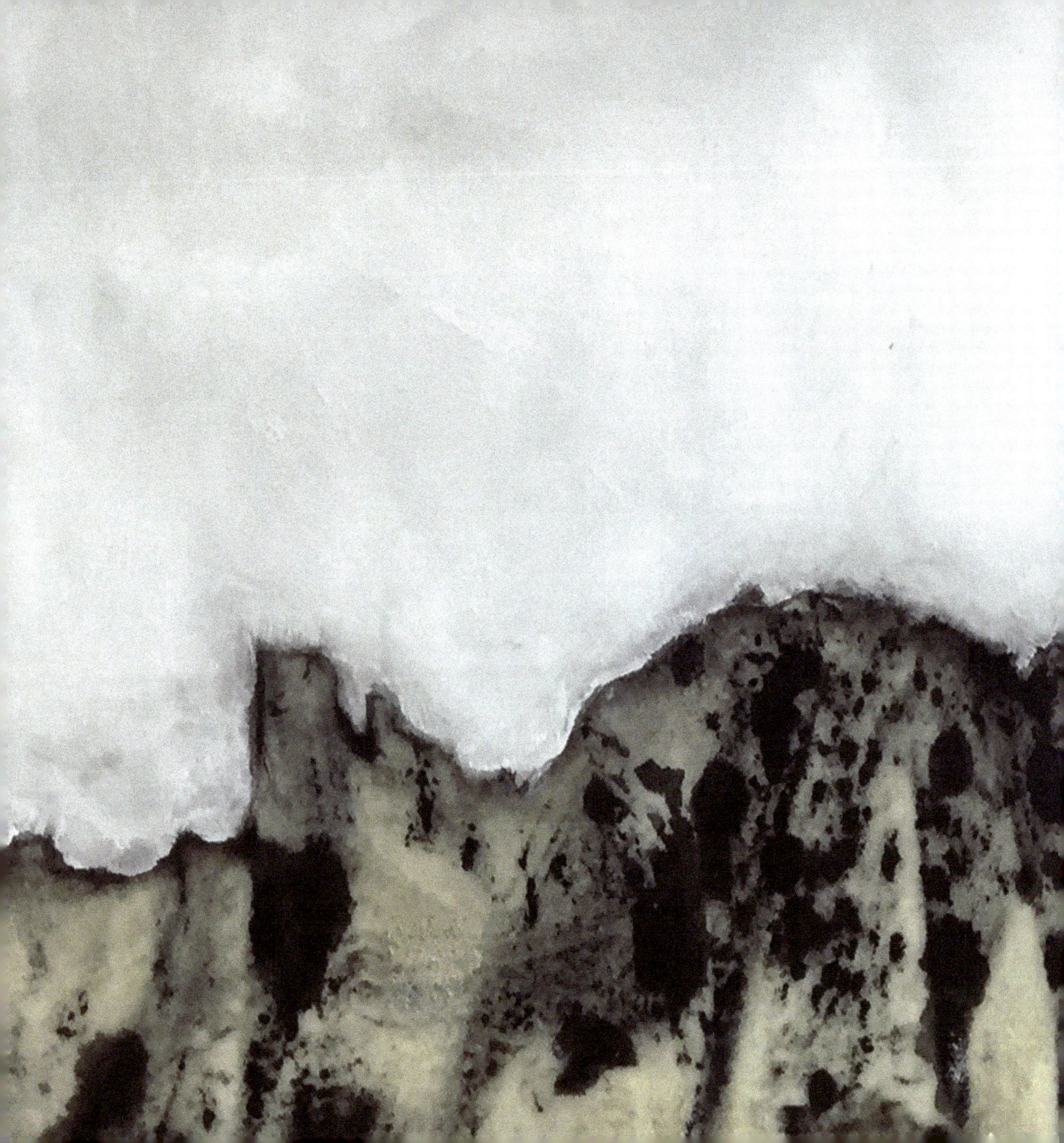

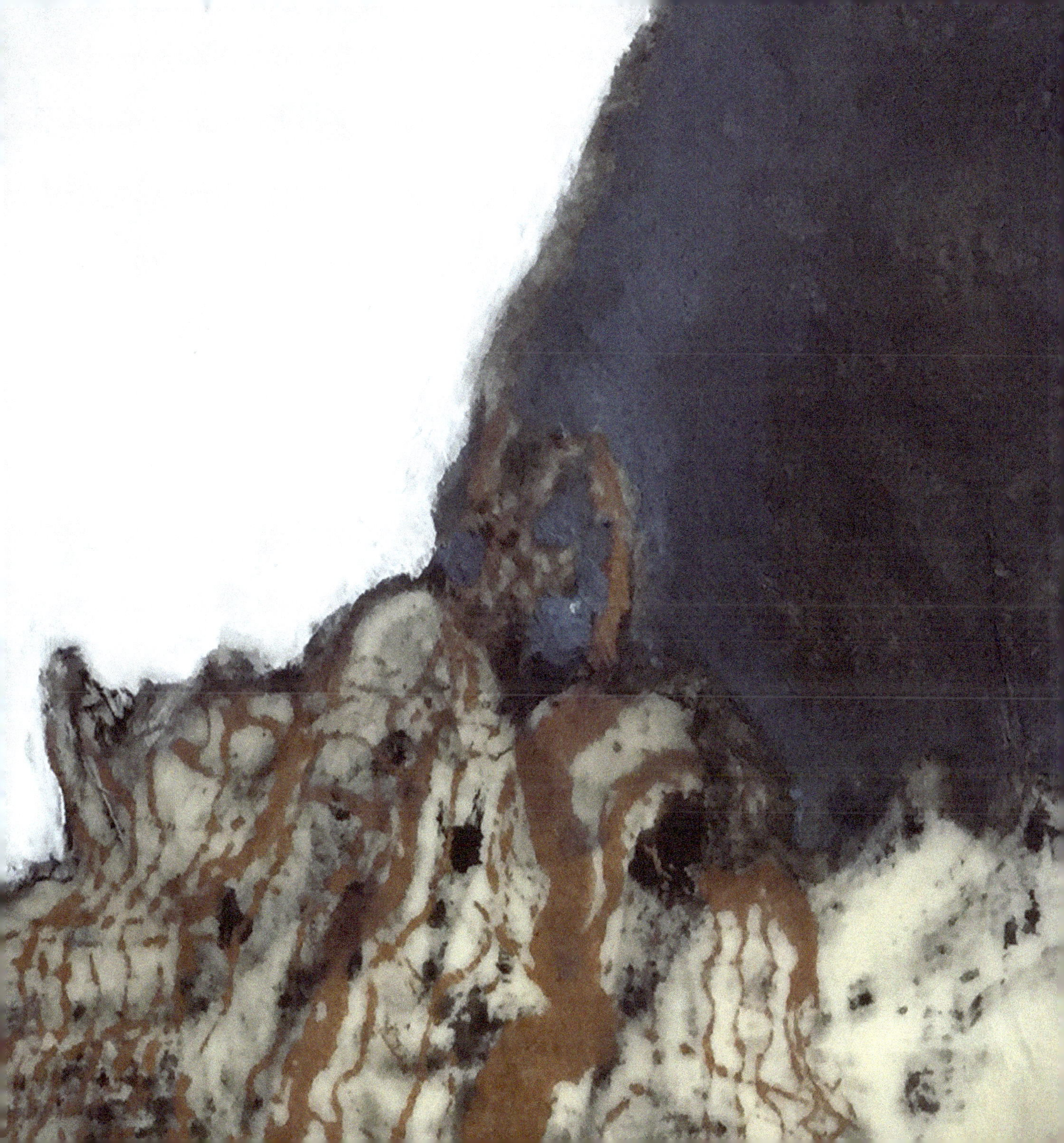

Root Cellar # 27
24" x 20" (61 x 50.8 cm)
2017

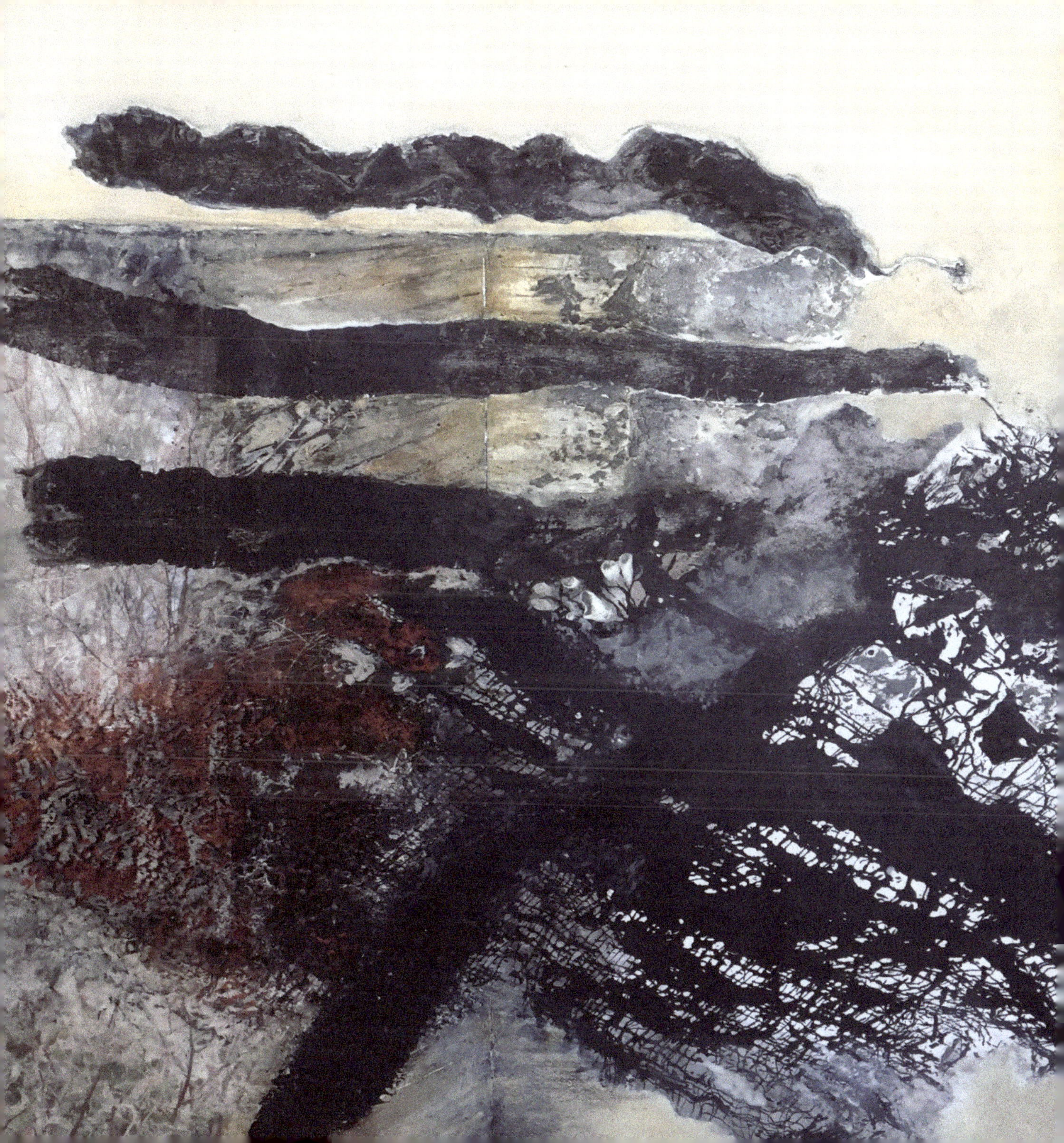

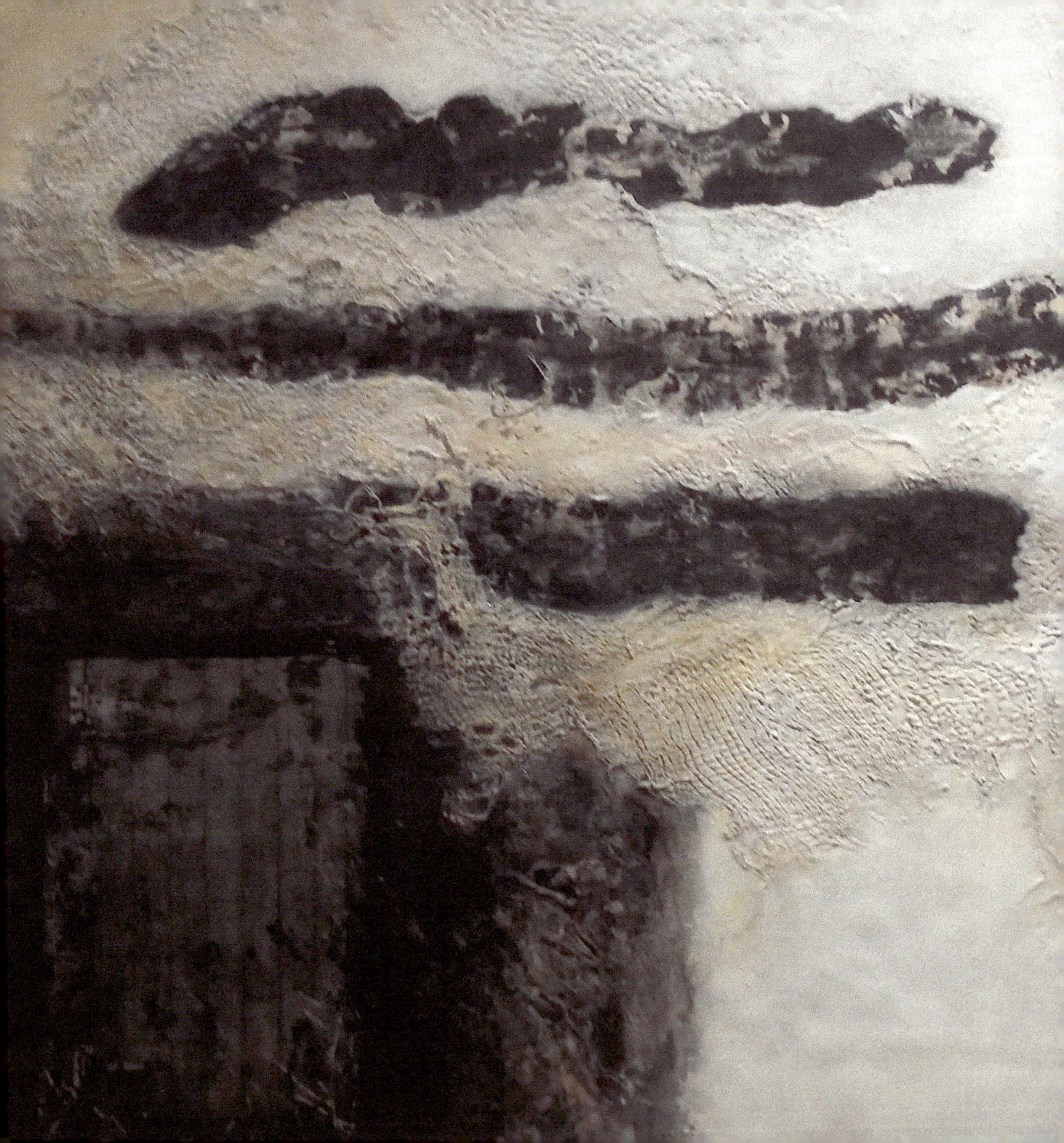

Root Cellar # 29
24" x 20" (61 x 50.8 cm)
2018

Root Cellar # 4
24" x 20" (61 x 50.8 cm)
2017

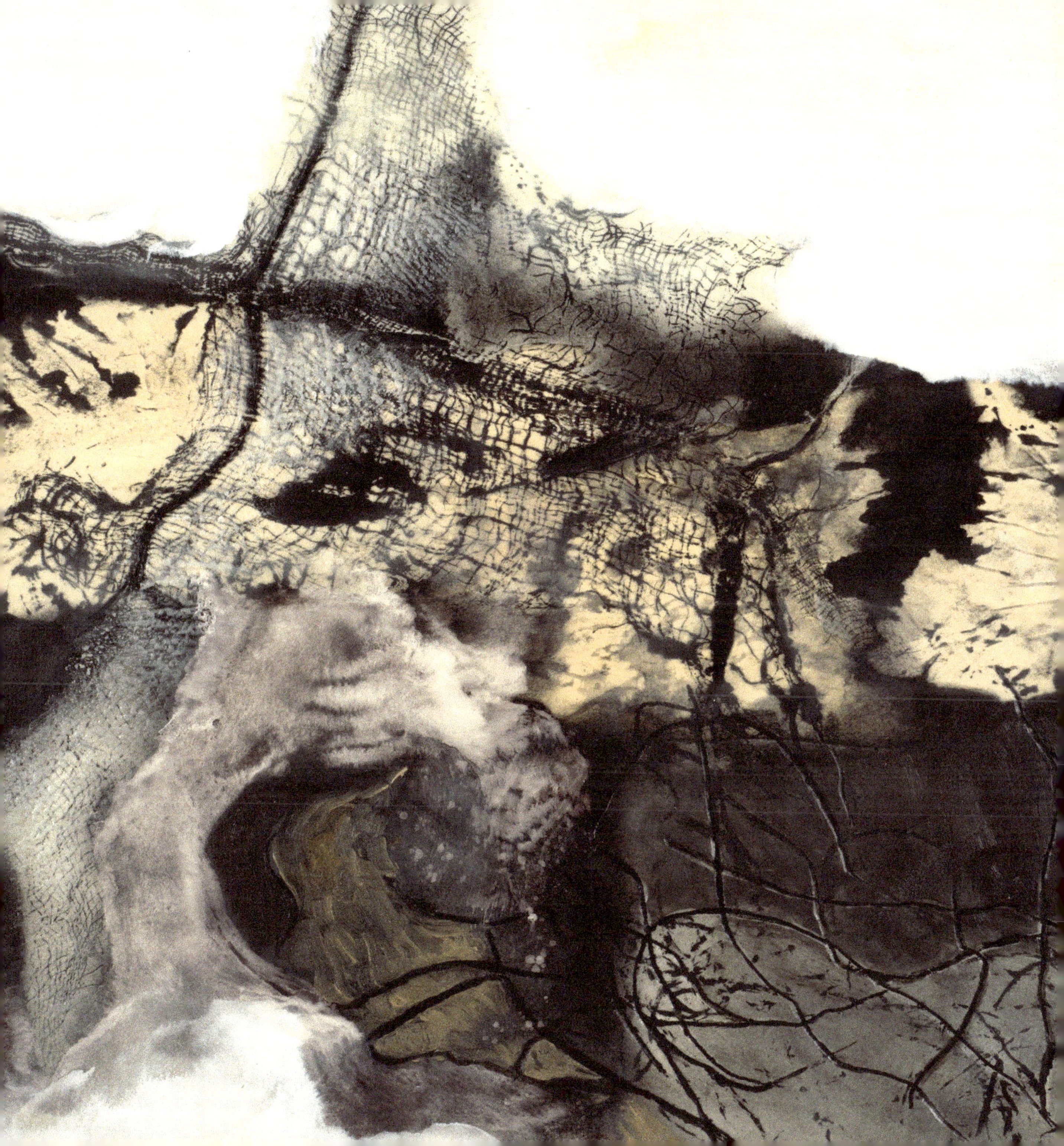

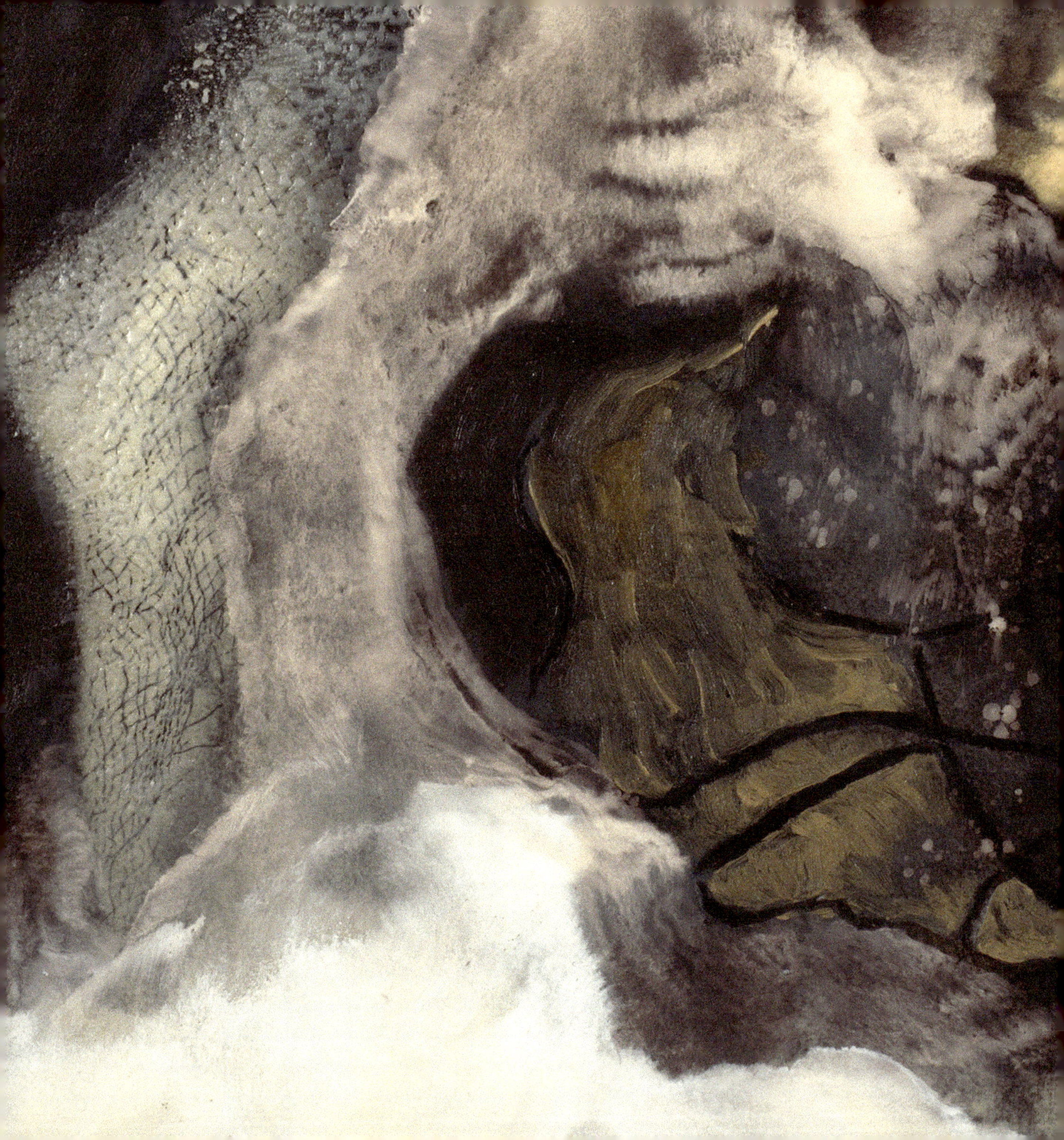

Root Cellar # 9
24″ x 20″ (61 x 50.8 cm)
2017

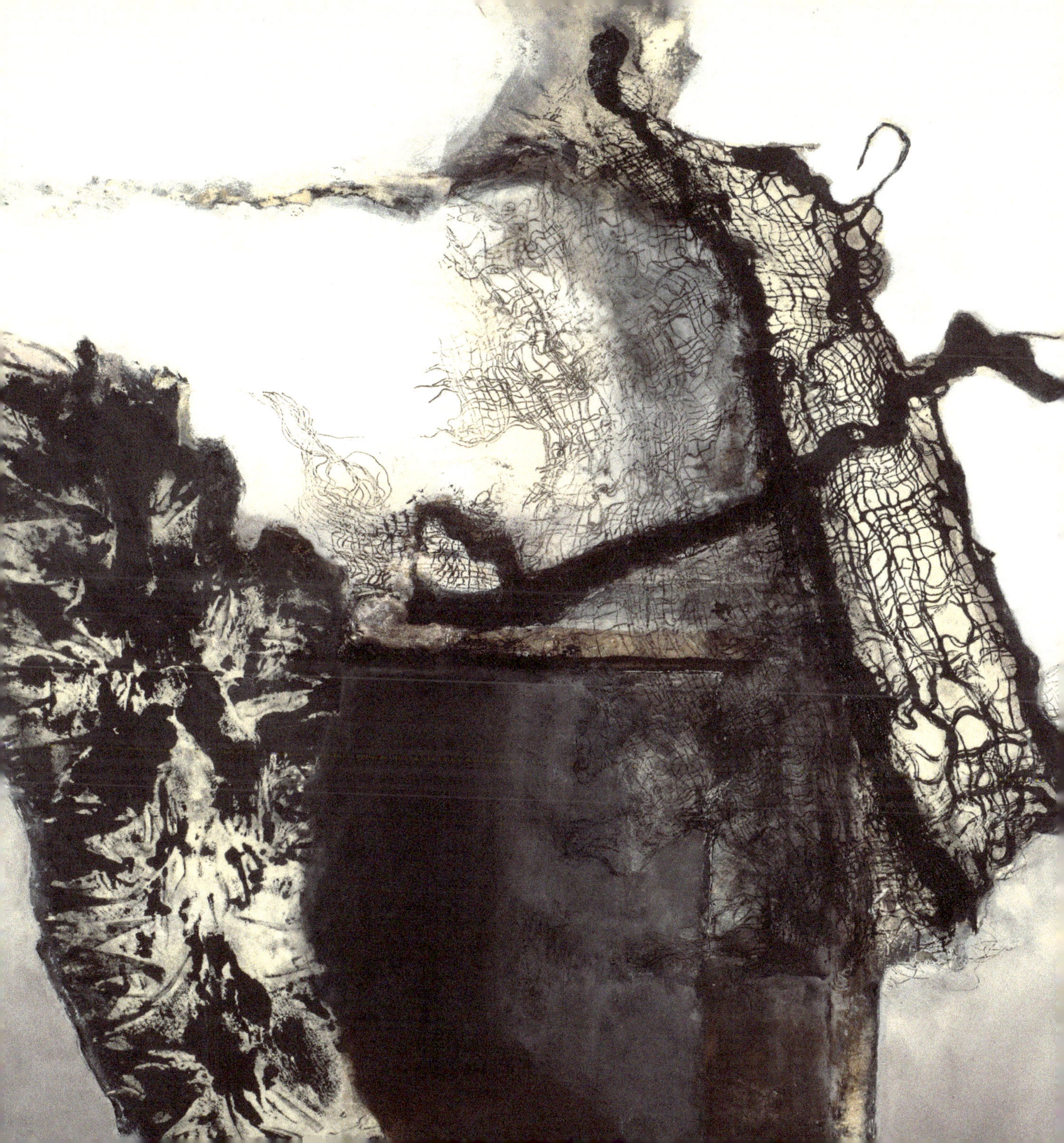

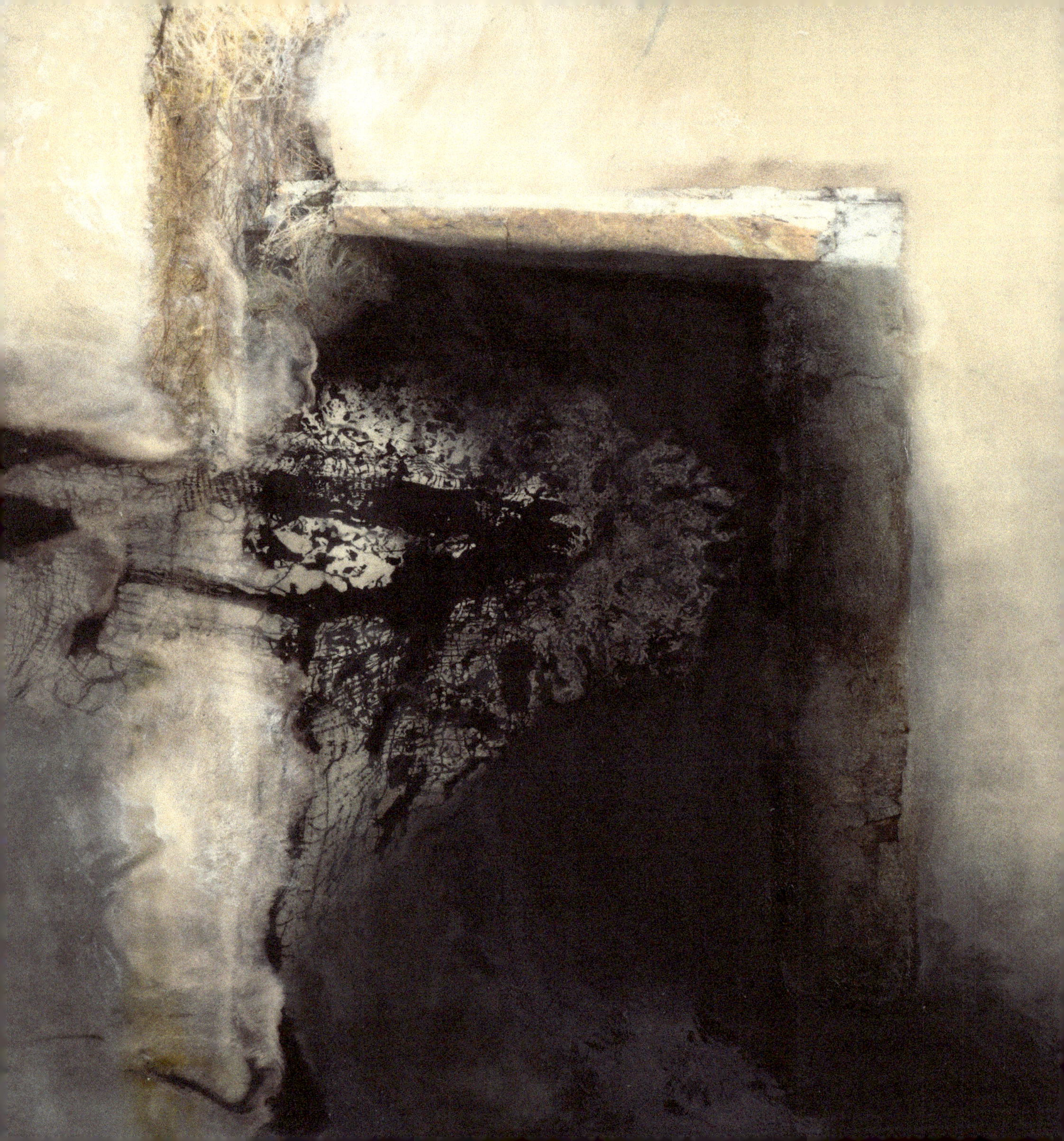

Root Cellar # 5
24" x 20" (61 x 50.8 cm)
2017

Root Cellar # 6
24" x 20" (61 x 50.8 cm)
2017

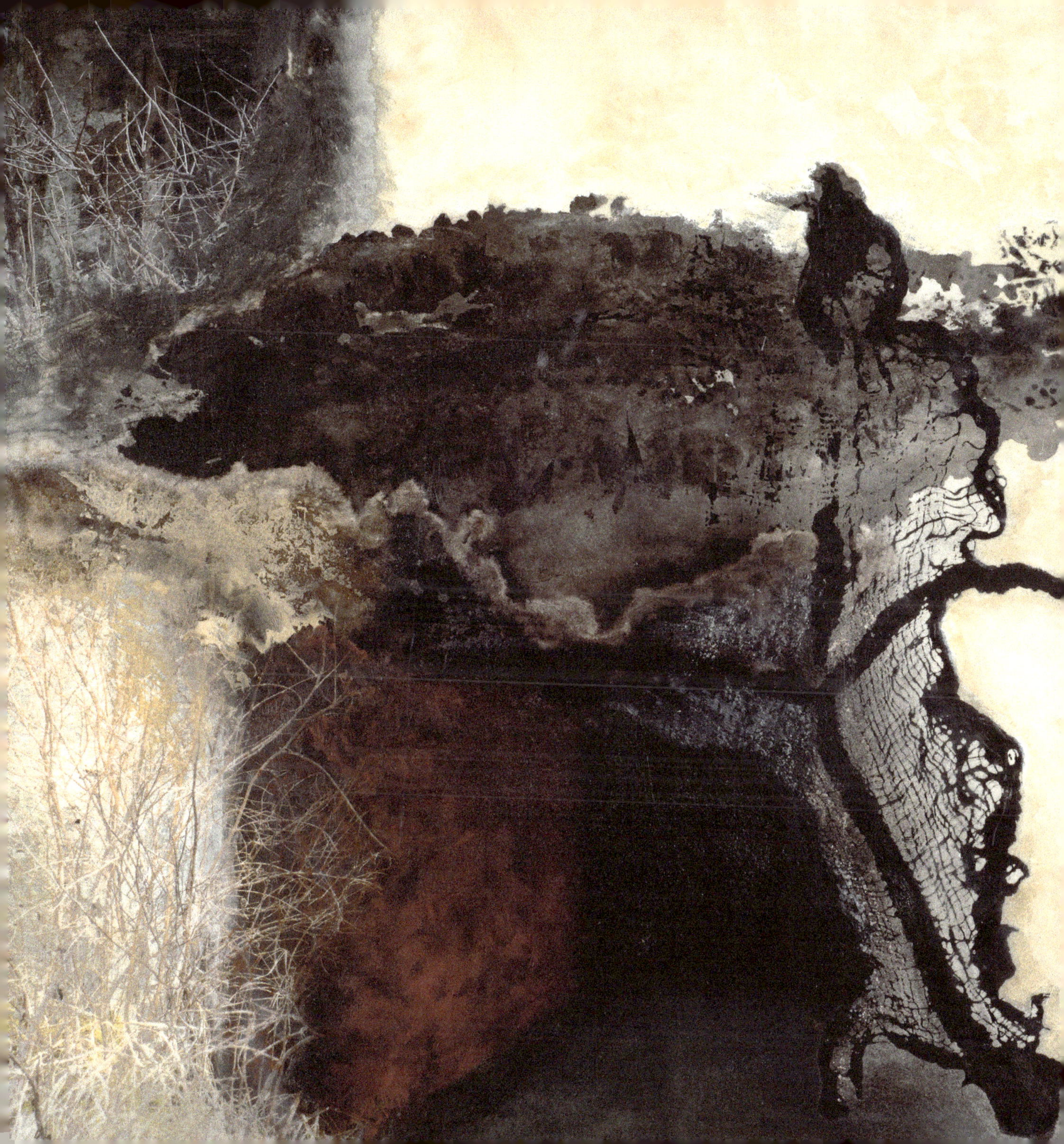

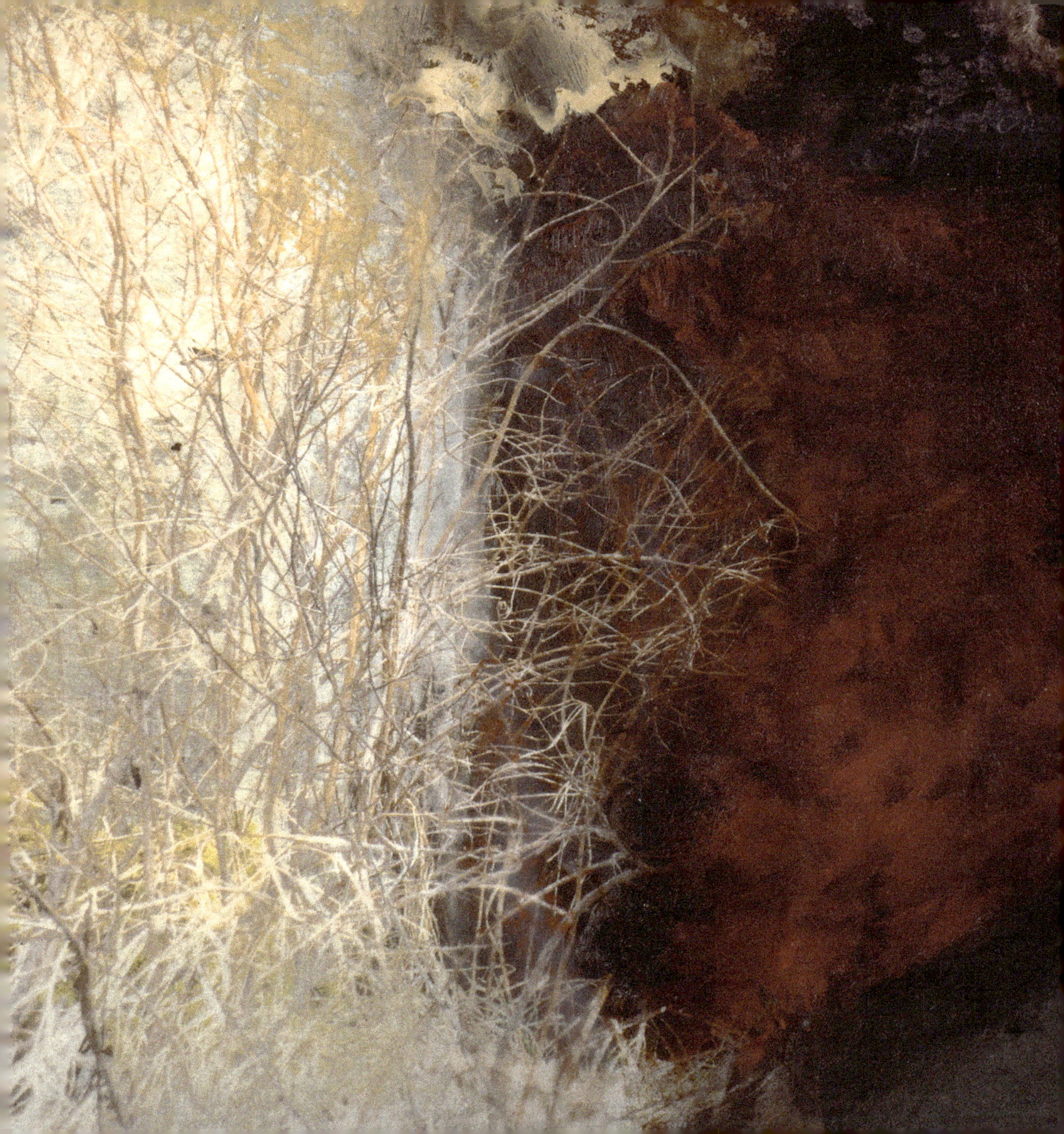

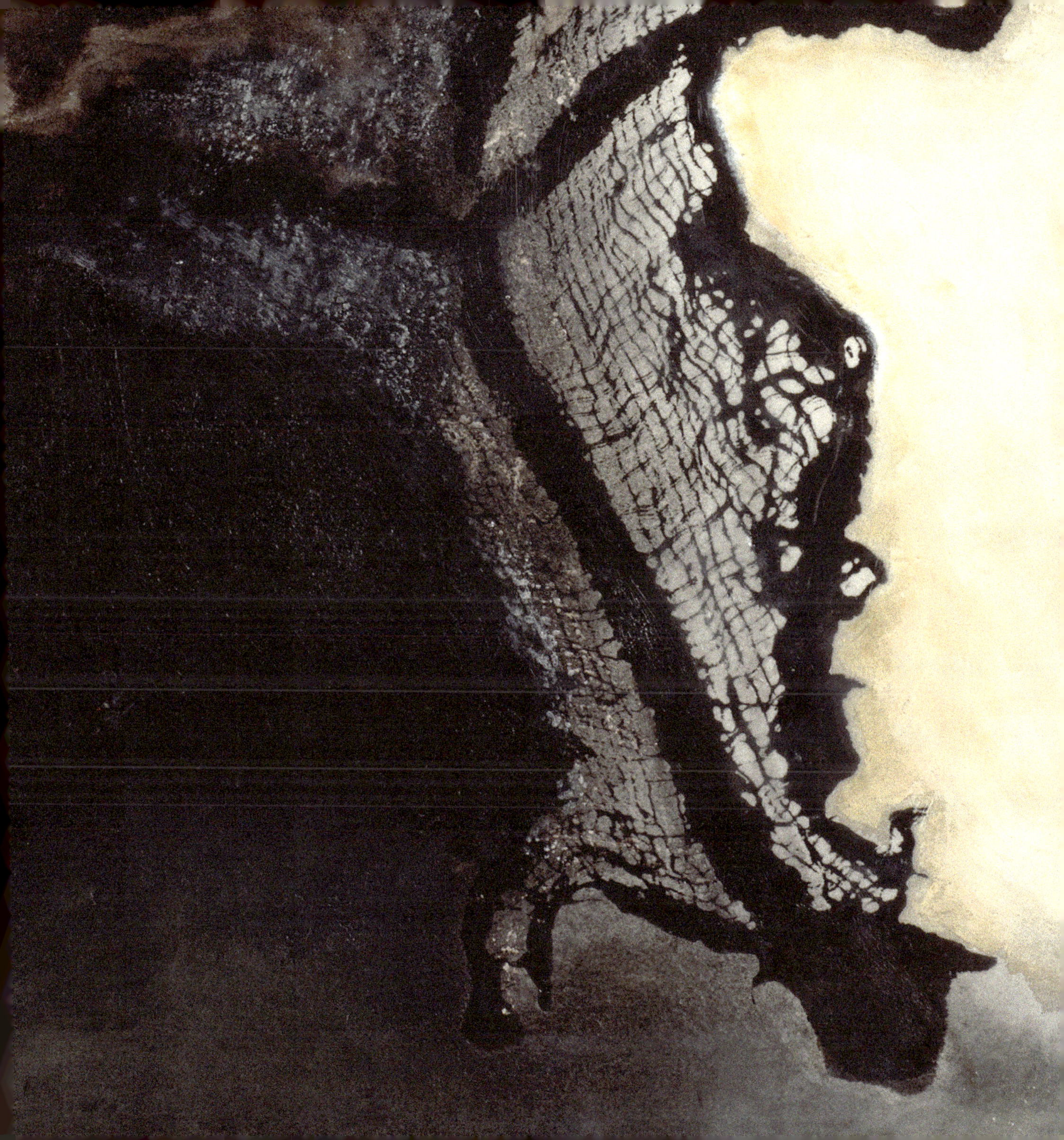

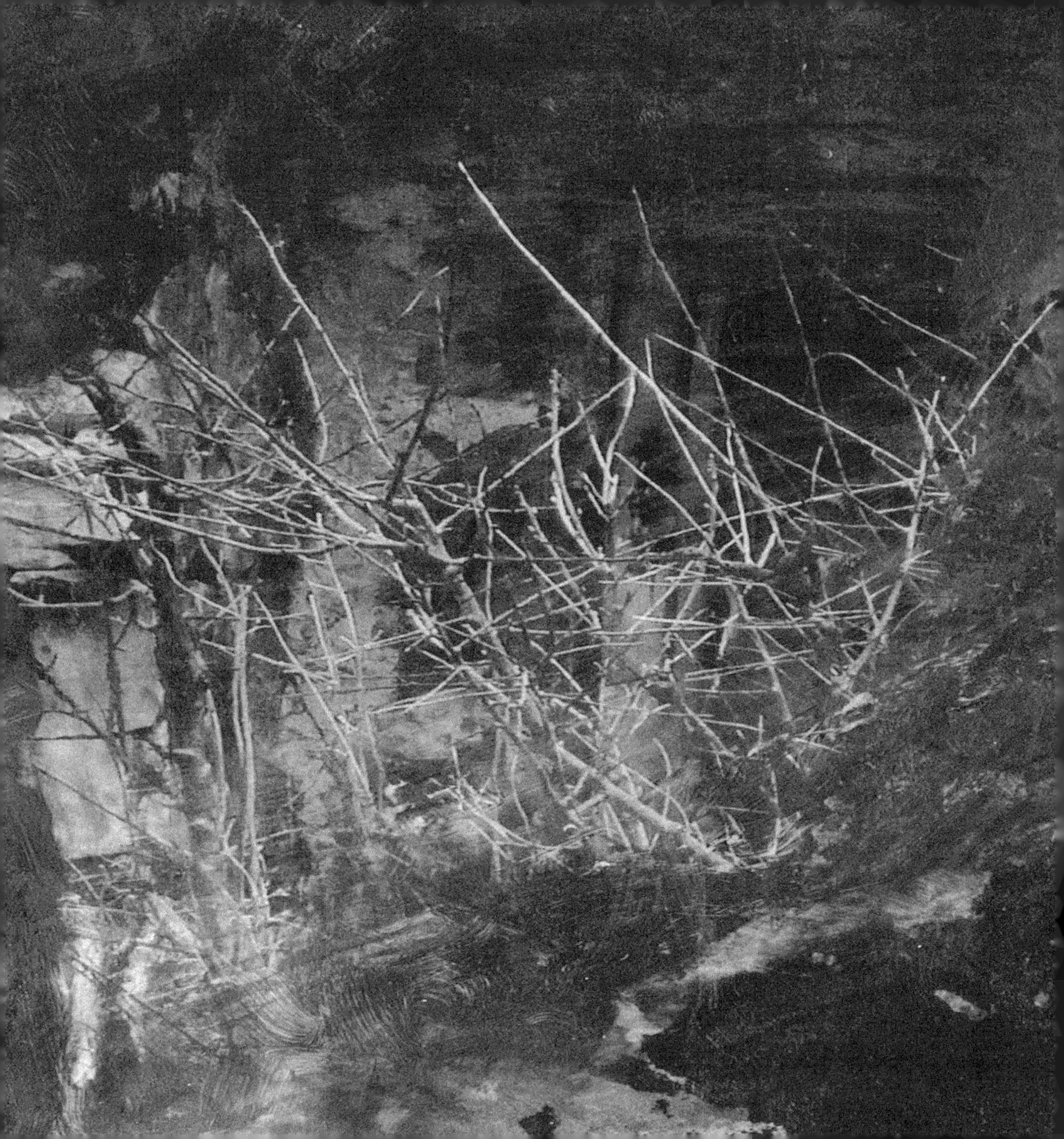

Root Cellar # 26
24" x 20" (61 x 50.8 cm)
2017

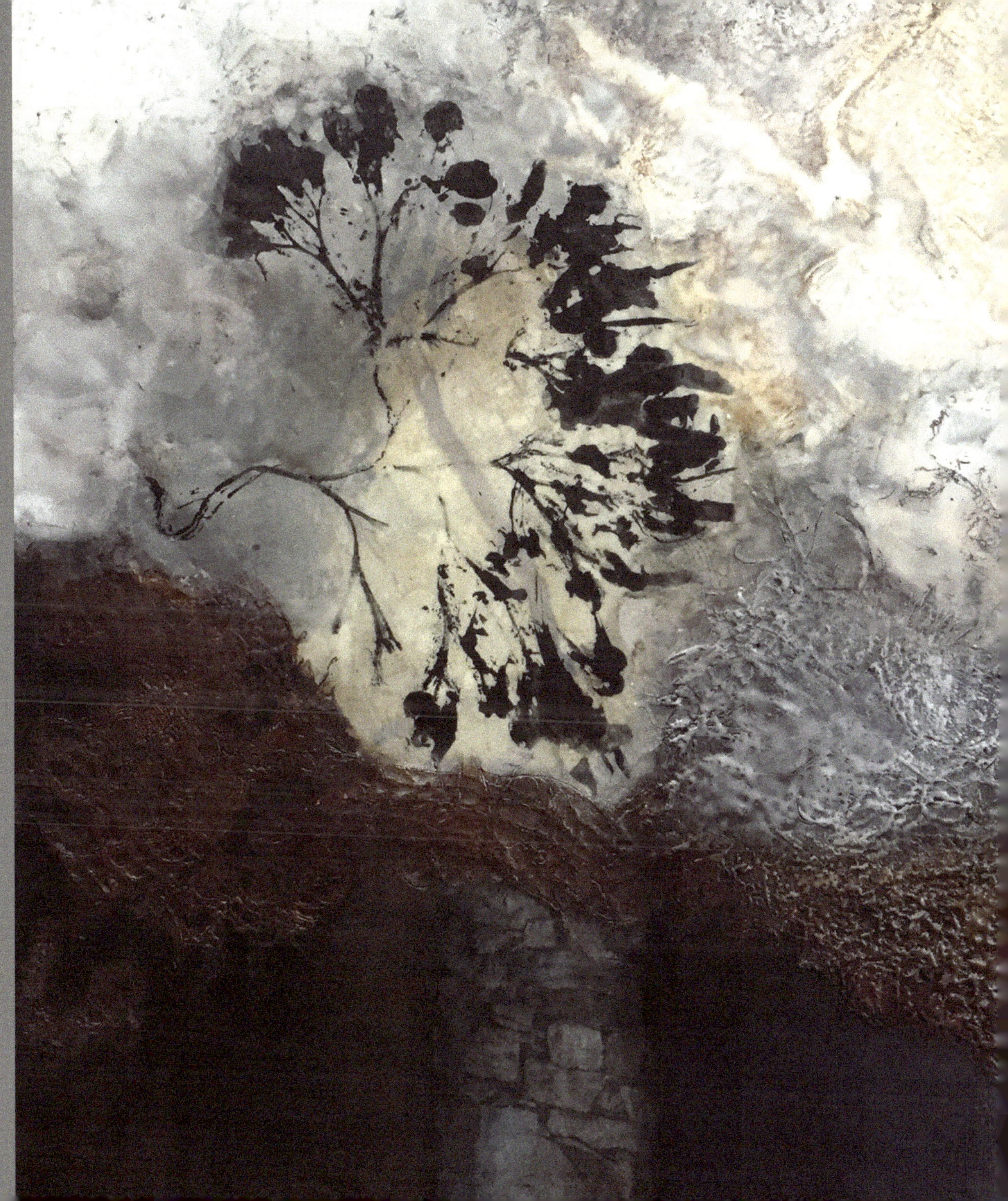

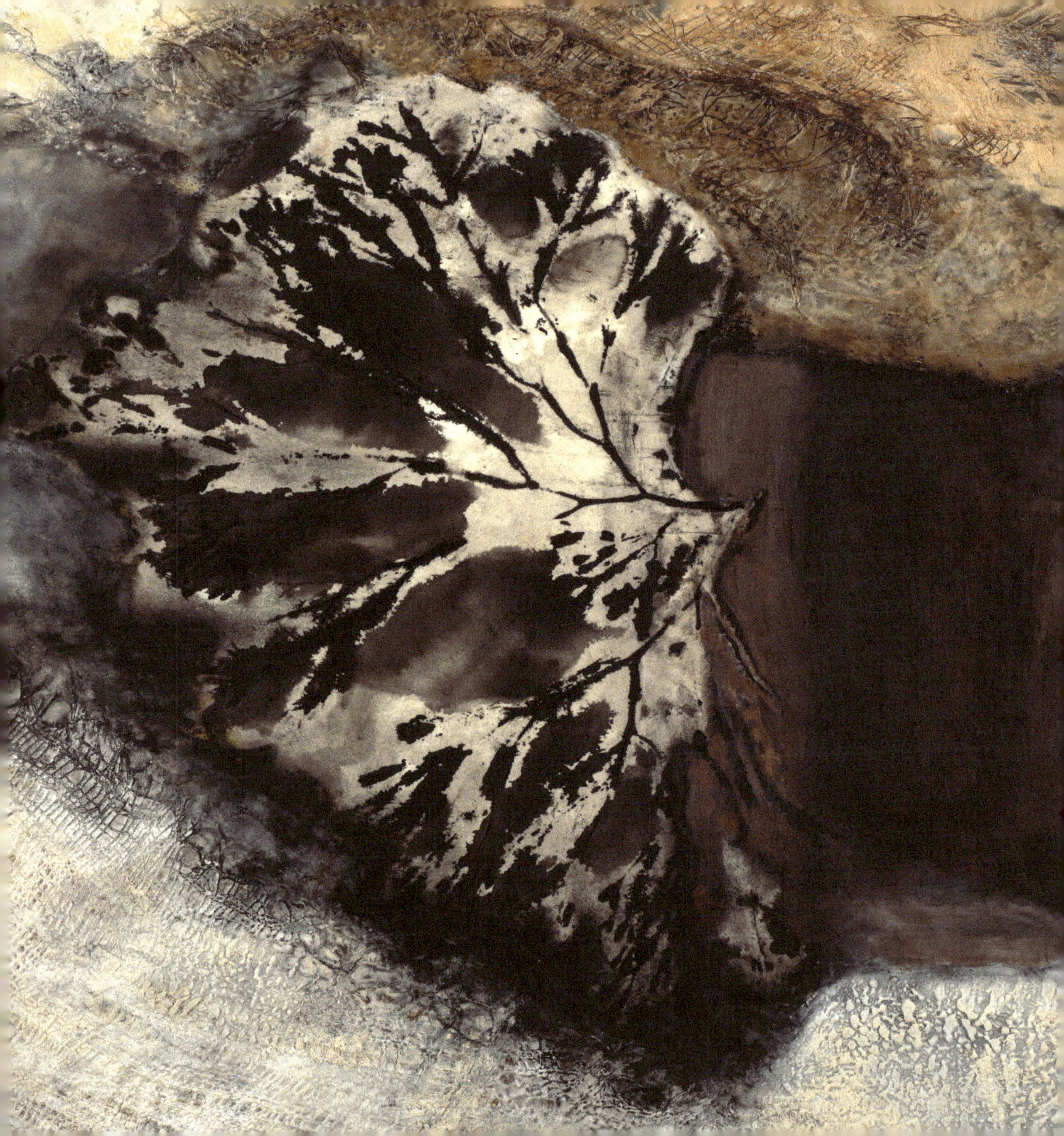

Root Cellar # 10
24" x 20" (61 x 50.8 cm)
2017

Root Cellar # 7
24" x 20" (61 x 50.8 cm)
2017

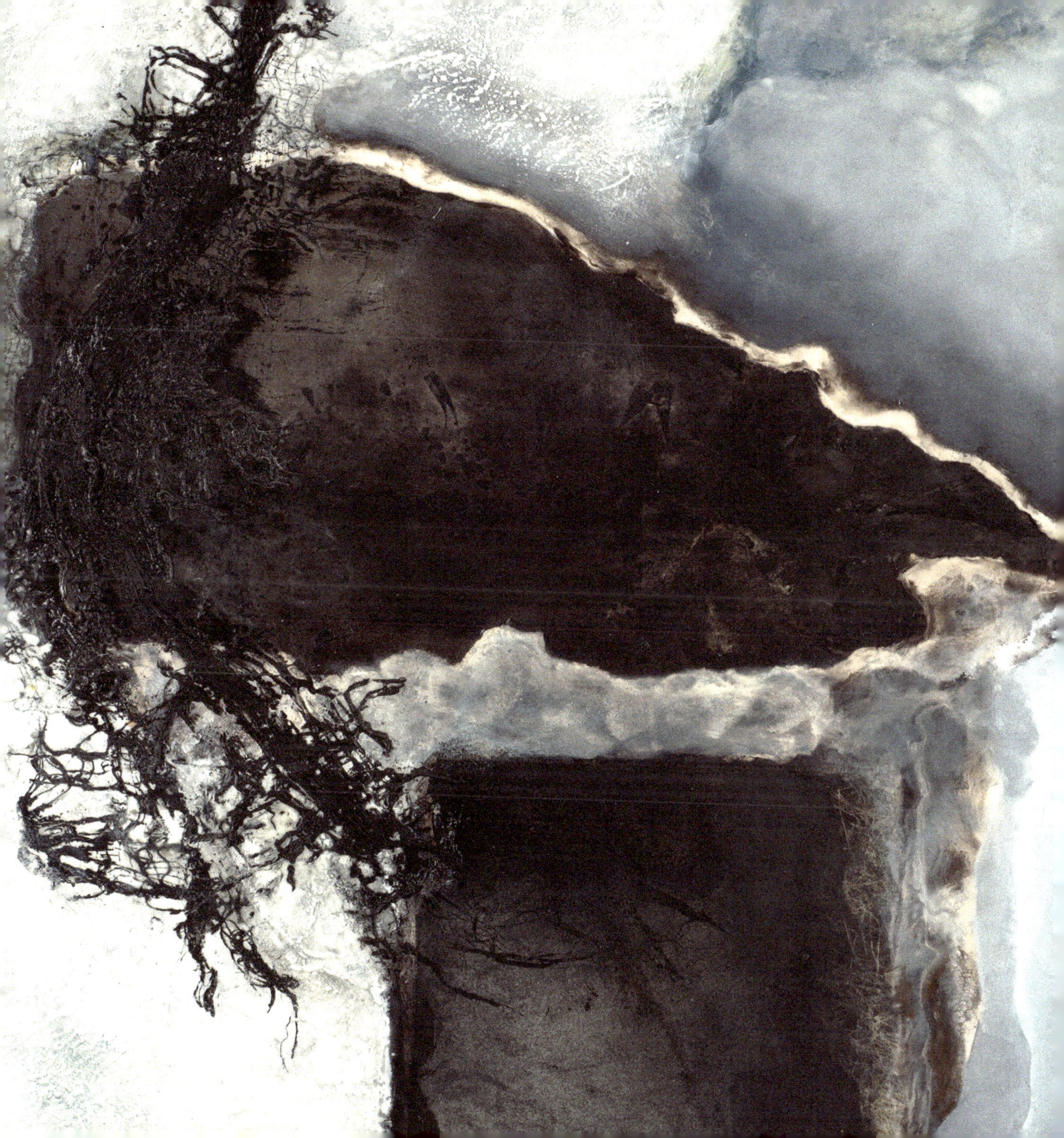

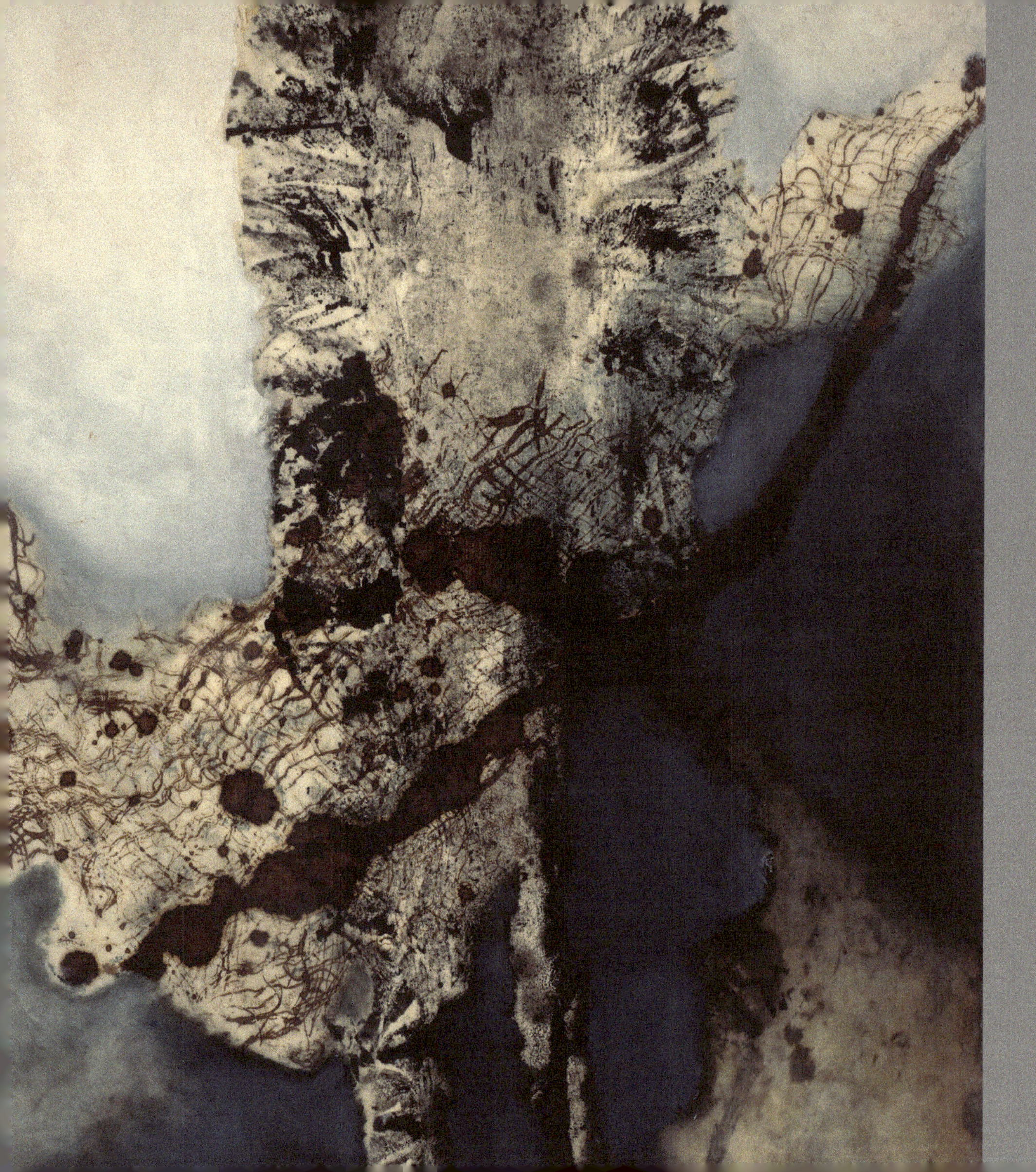

Root Cellar # 11
20" x 17" (50.8 x 43.2 cm)
2017

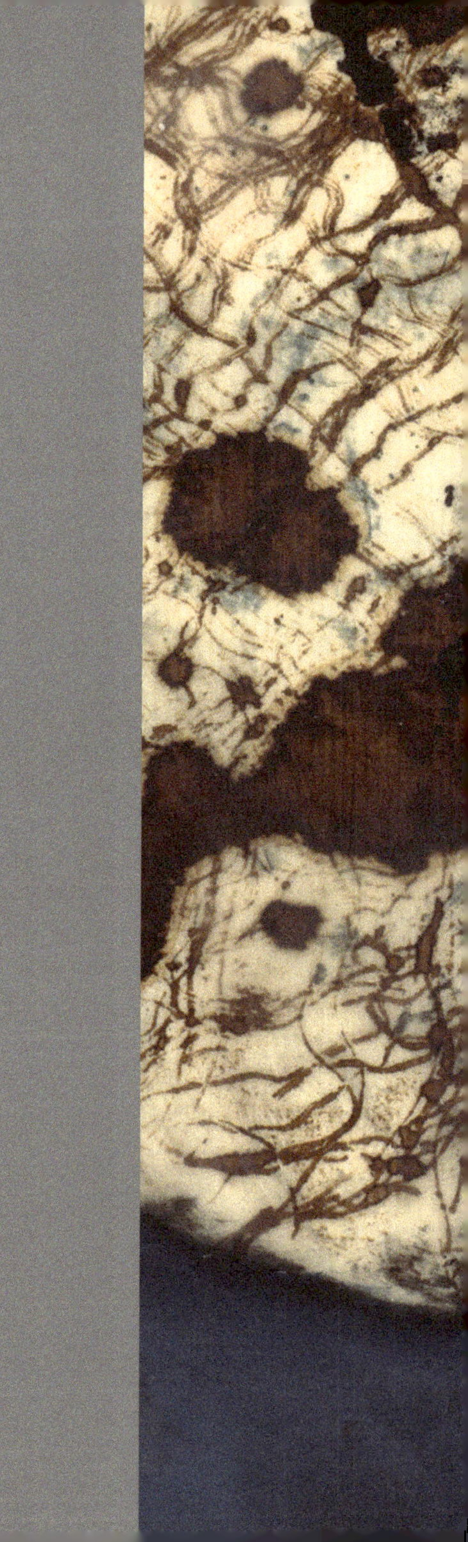

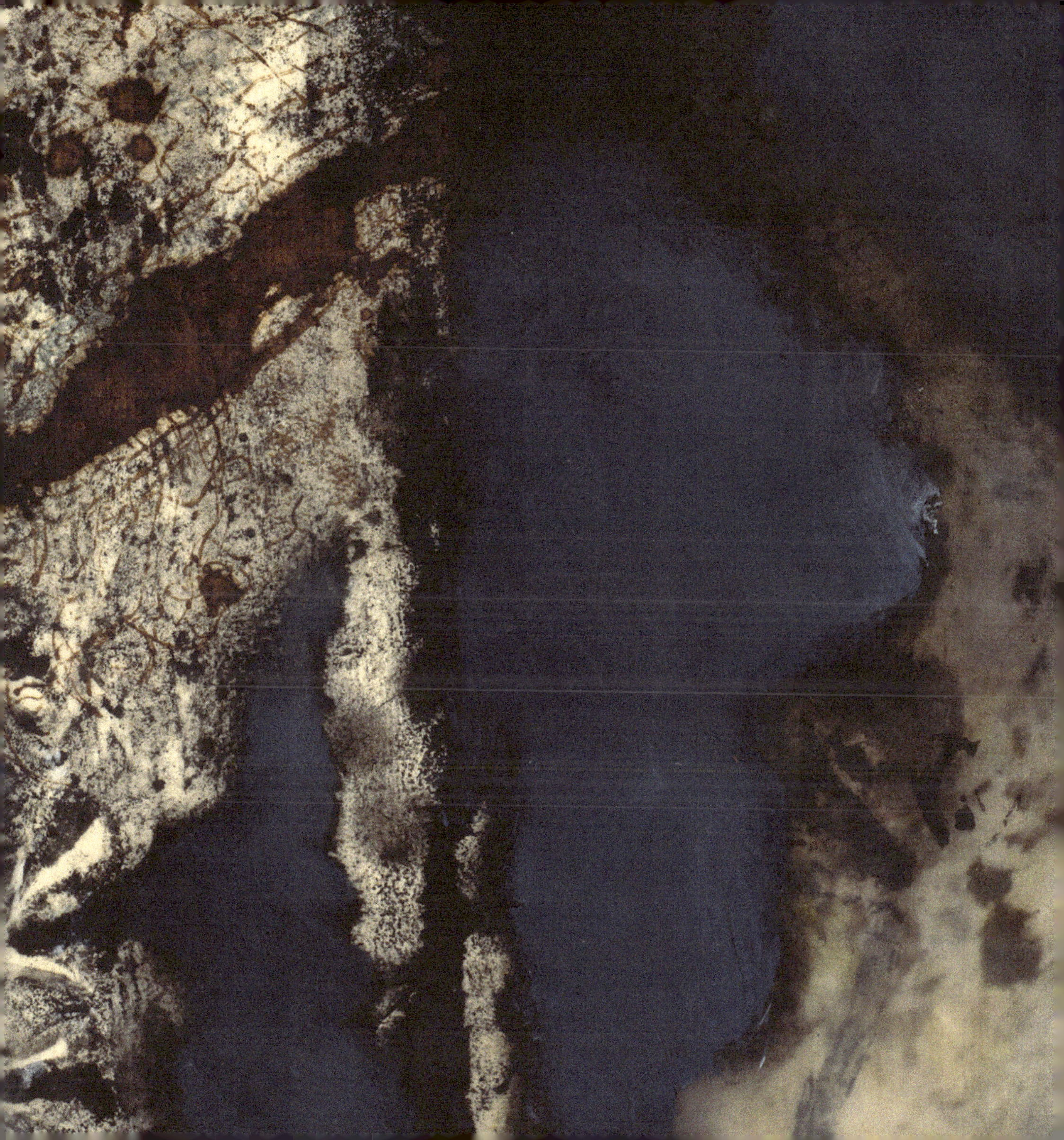

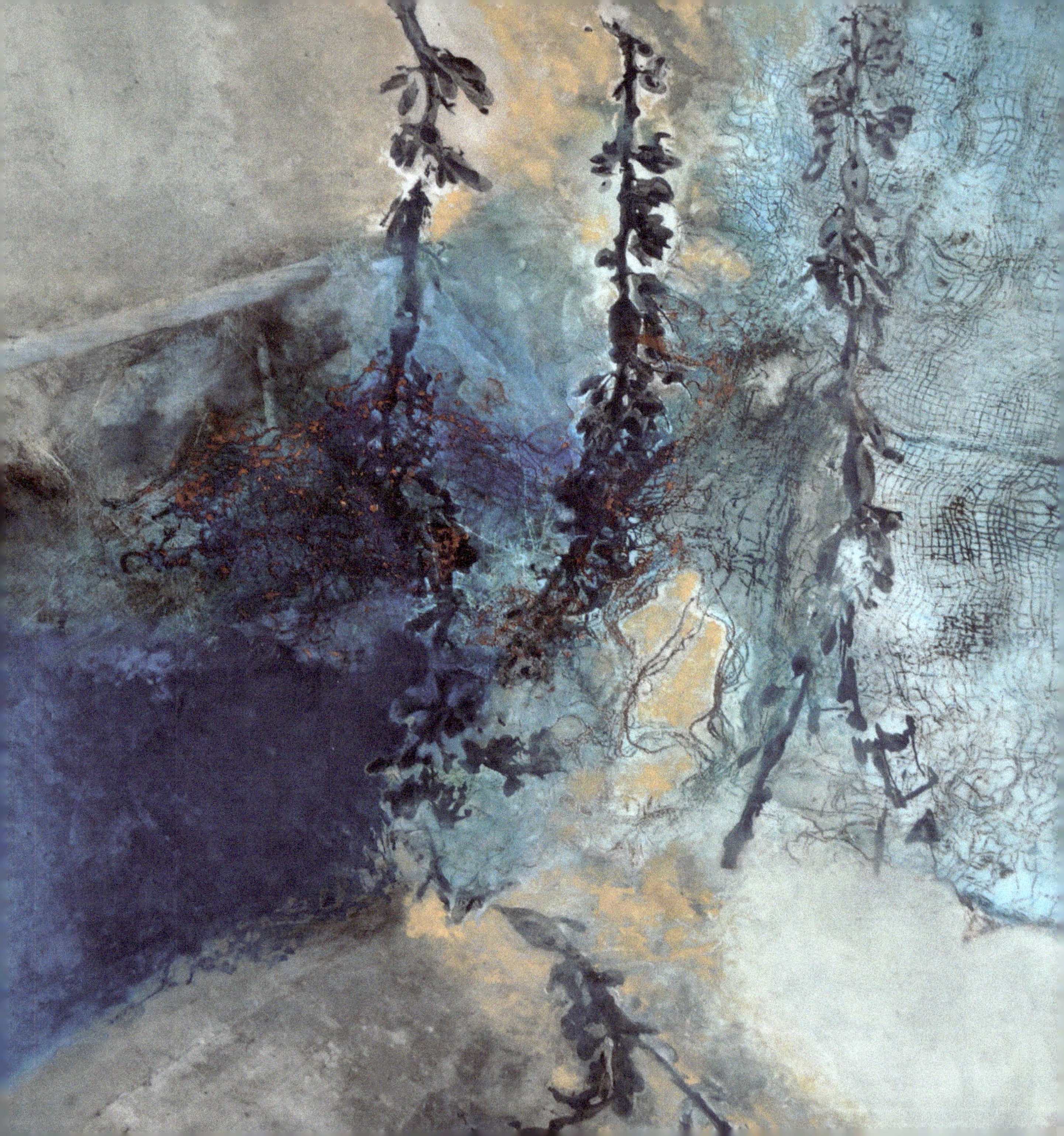

Root Cellar # 18
24" x 20" (61 x 50.8 cm)
2017

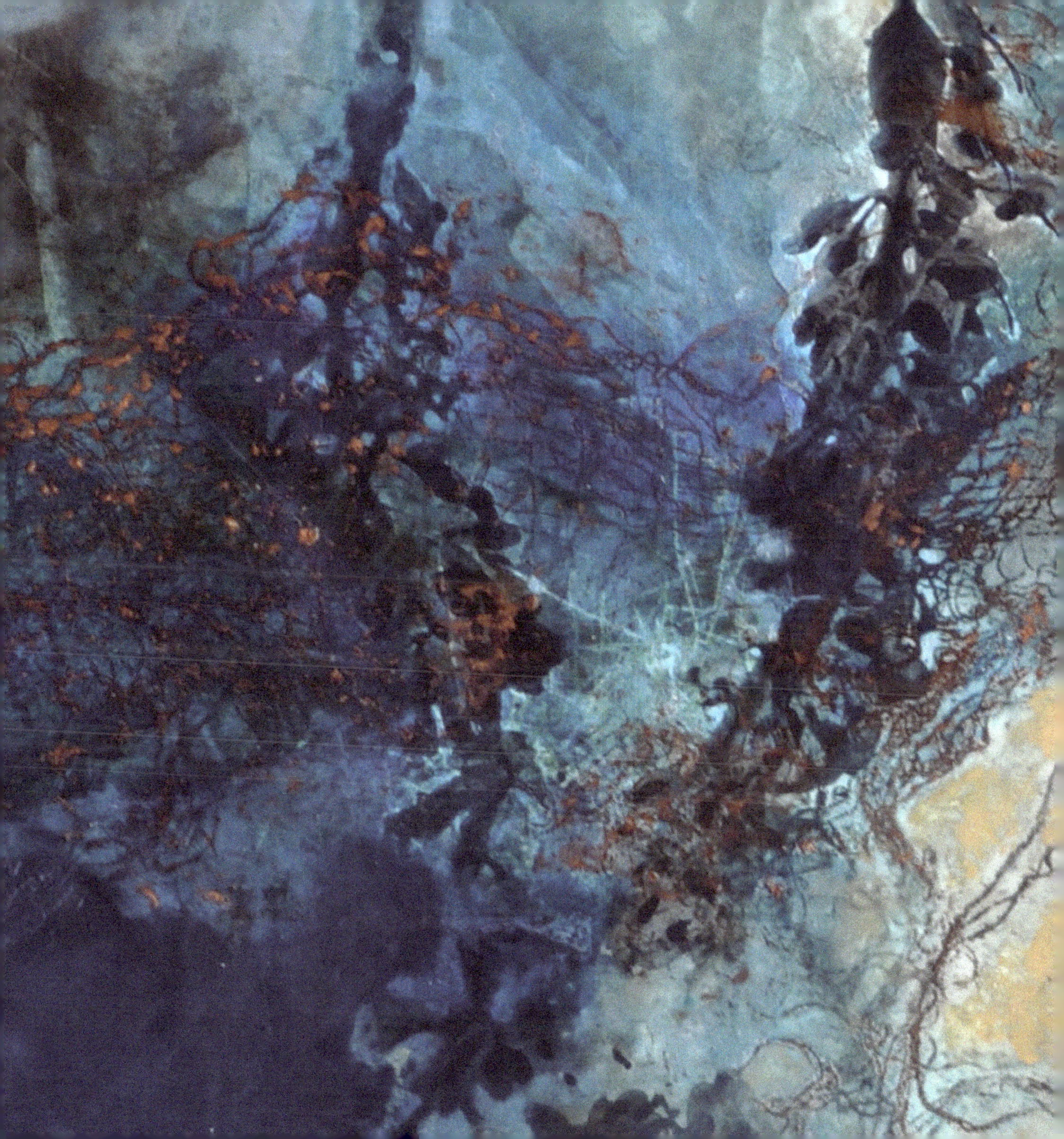

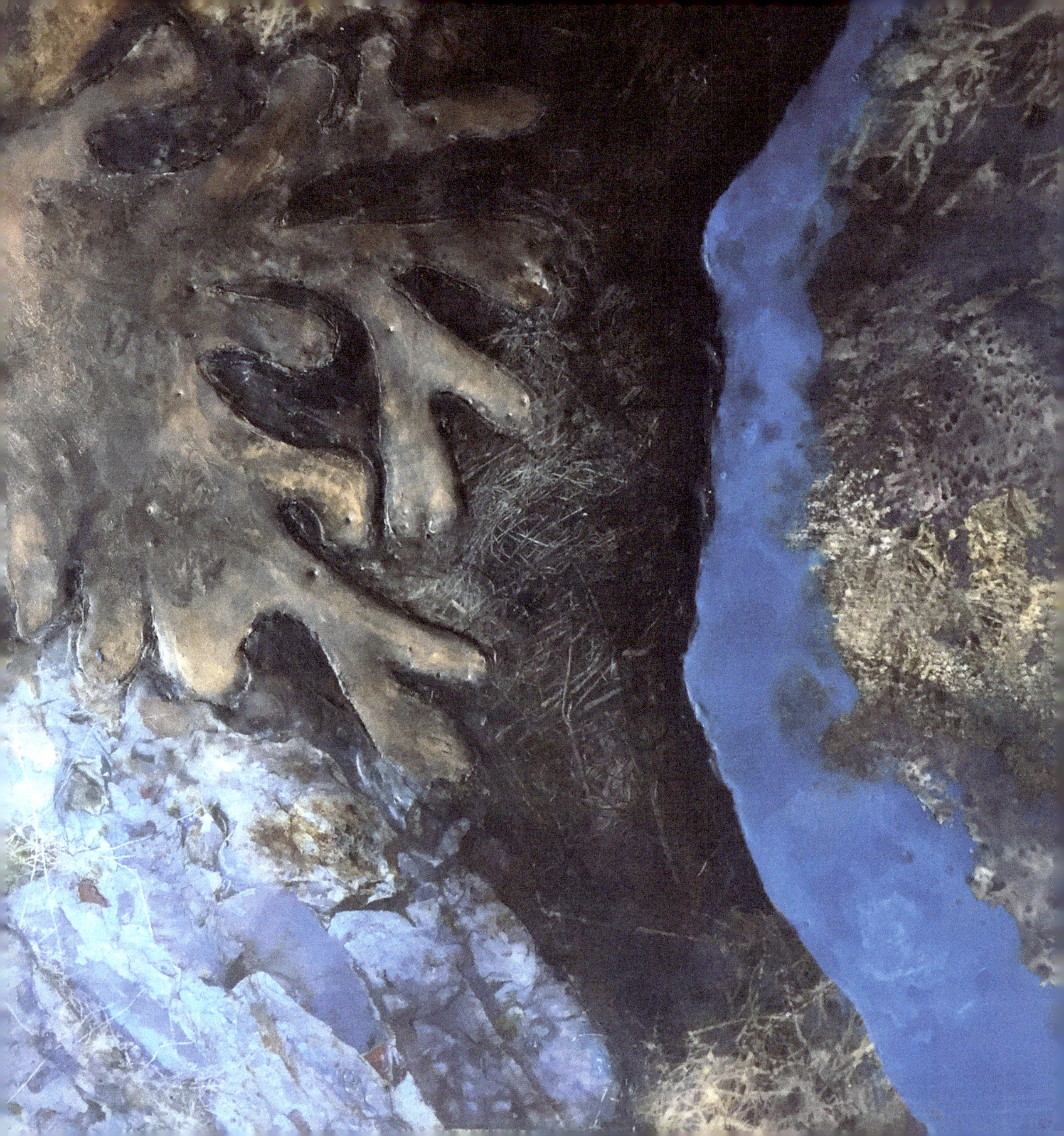

Root Cellar # 24
10" x 10" (25.4 x 25.4 cm)
2018

Root Cellar # 23
12" x 12" (30.5 x 30.5 cm)
2017

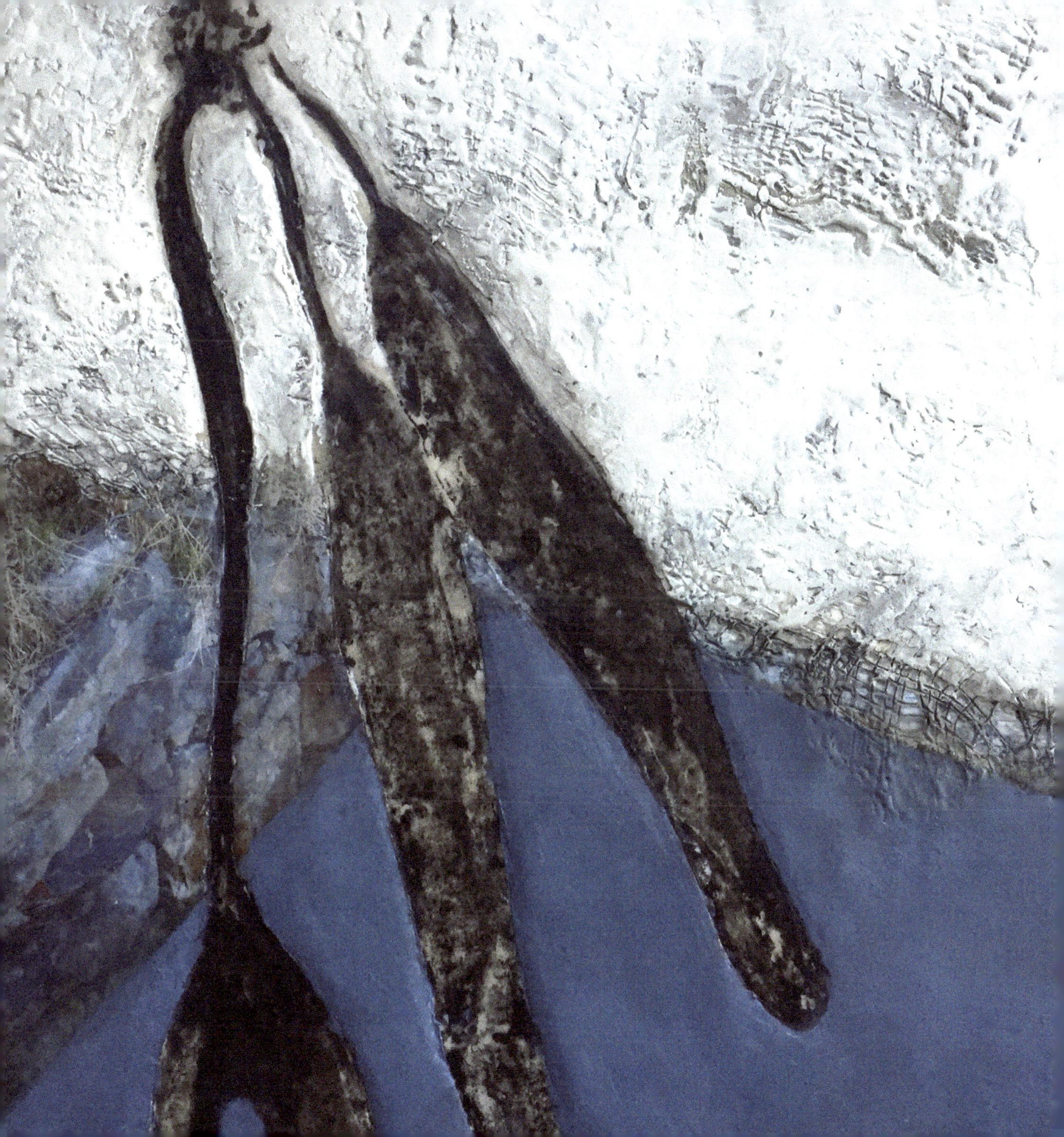

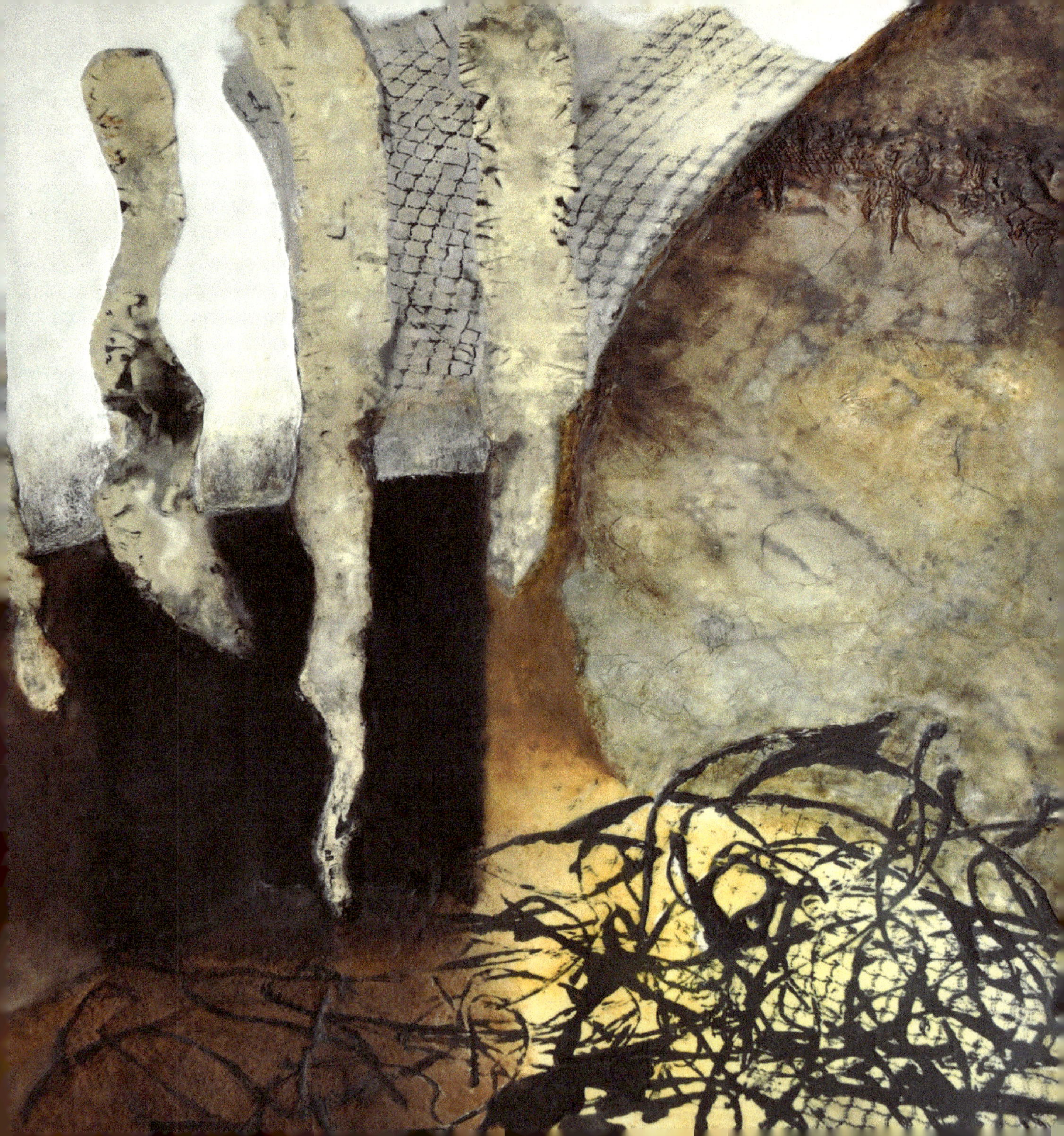

Root Cellar # 16
26" x 20" (66 x 50.8 cm)
2017

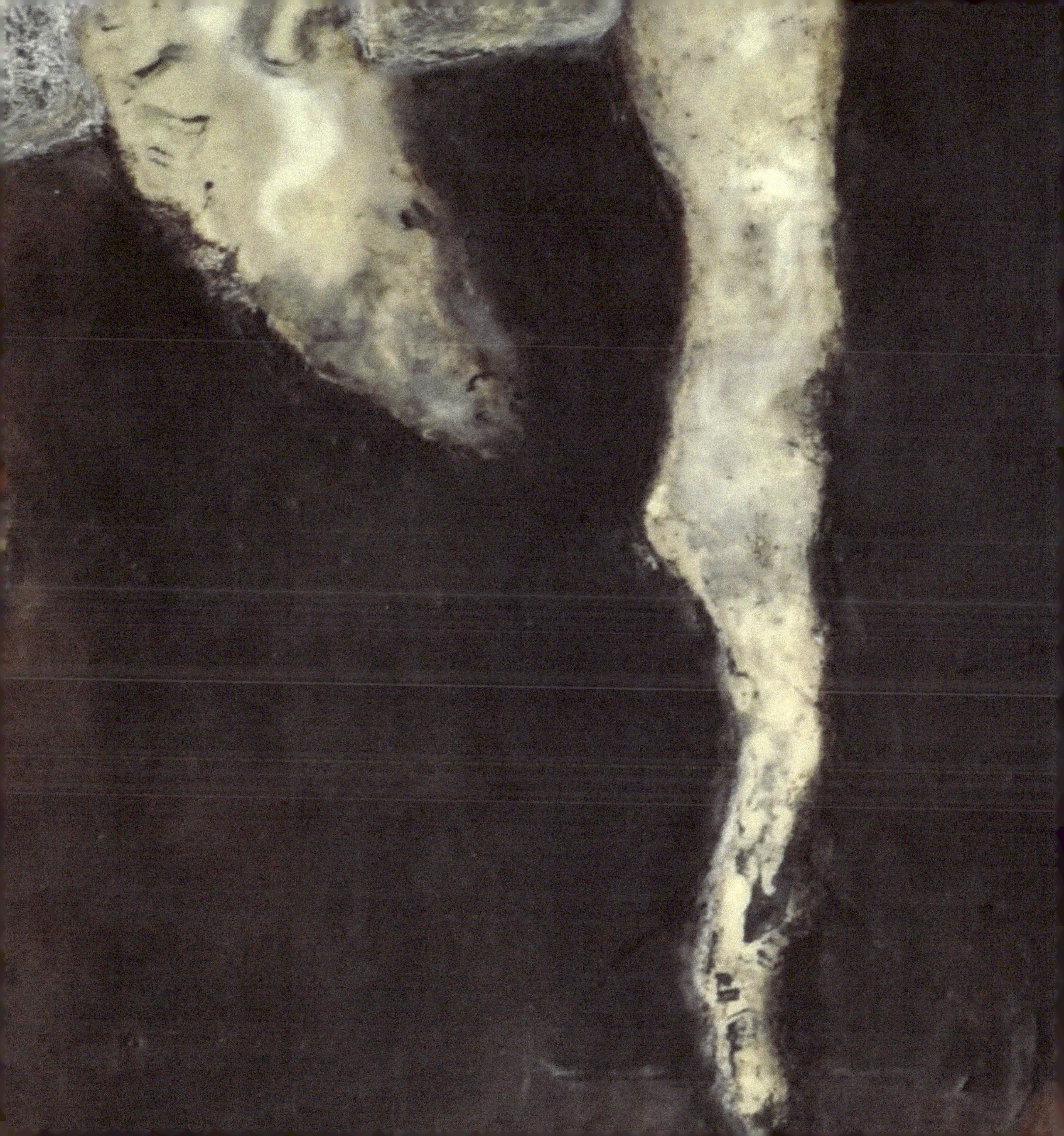

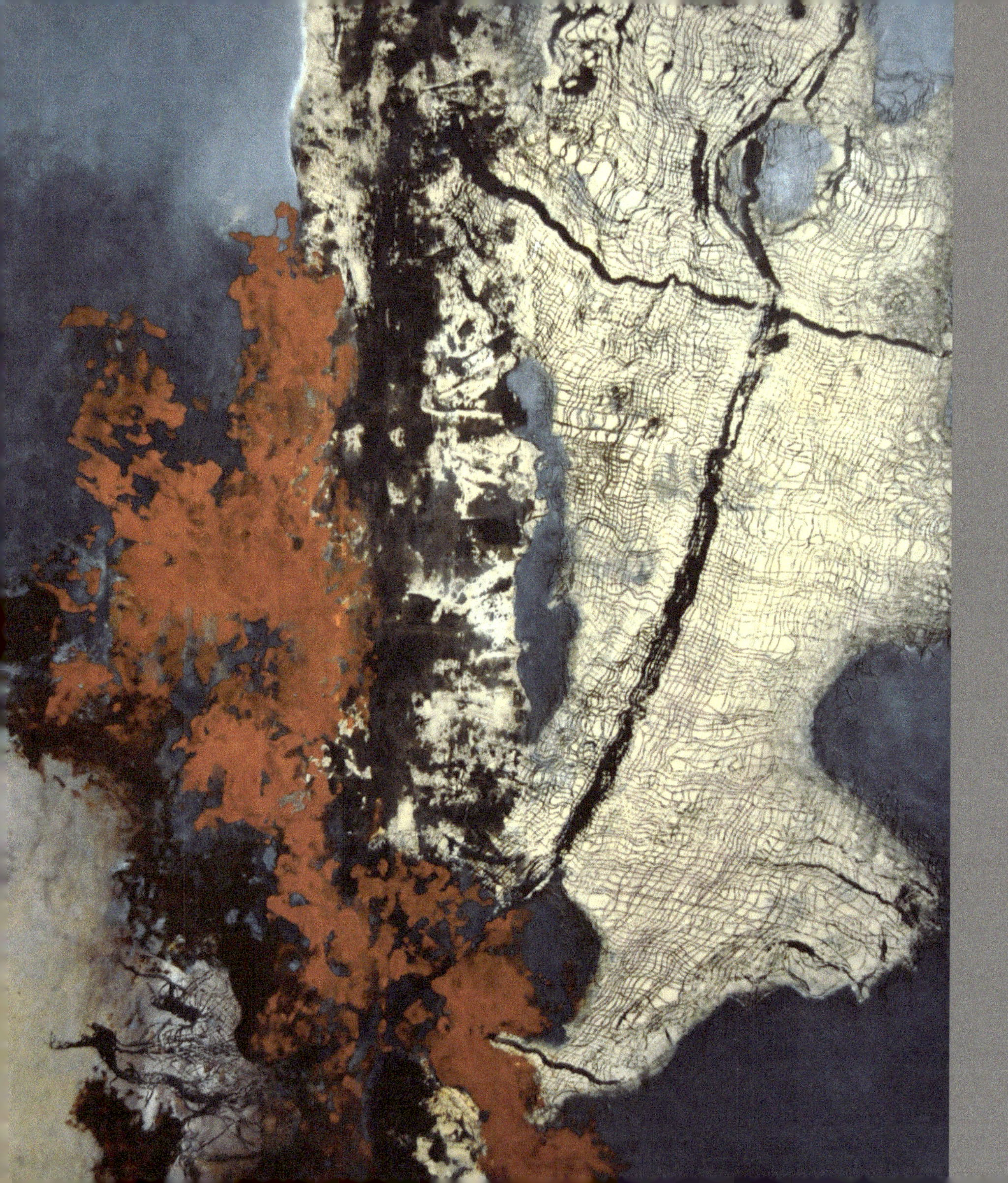

Root Cellar # 21
33″ x 26″ (83.8 x 66 cm)
2017

Root Cellar # 17
26″ x 20″ (66 x 50.8 cm)
2017

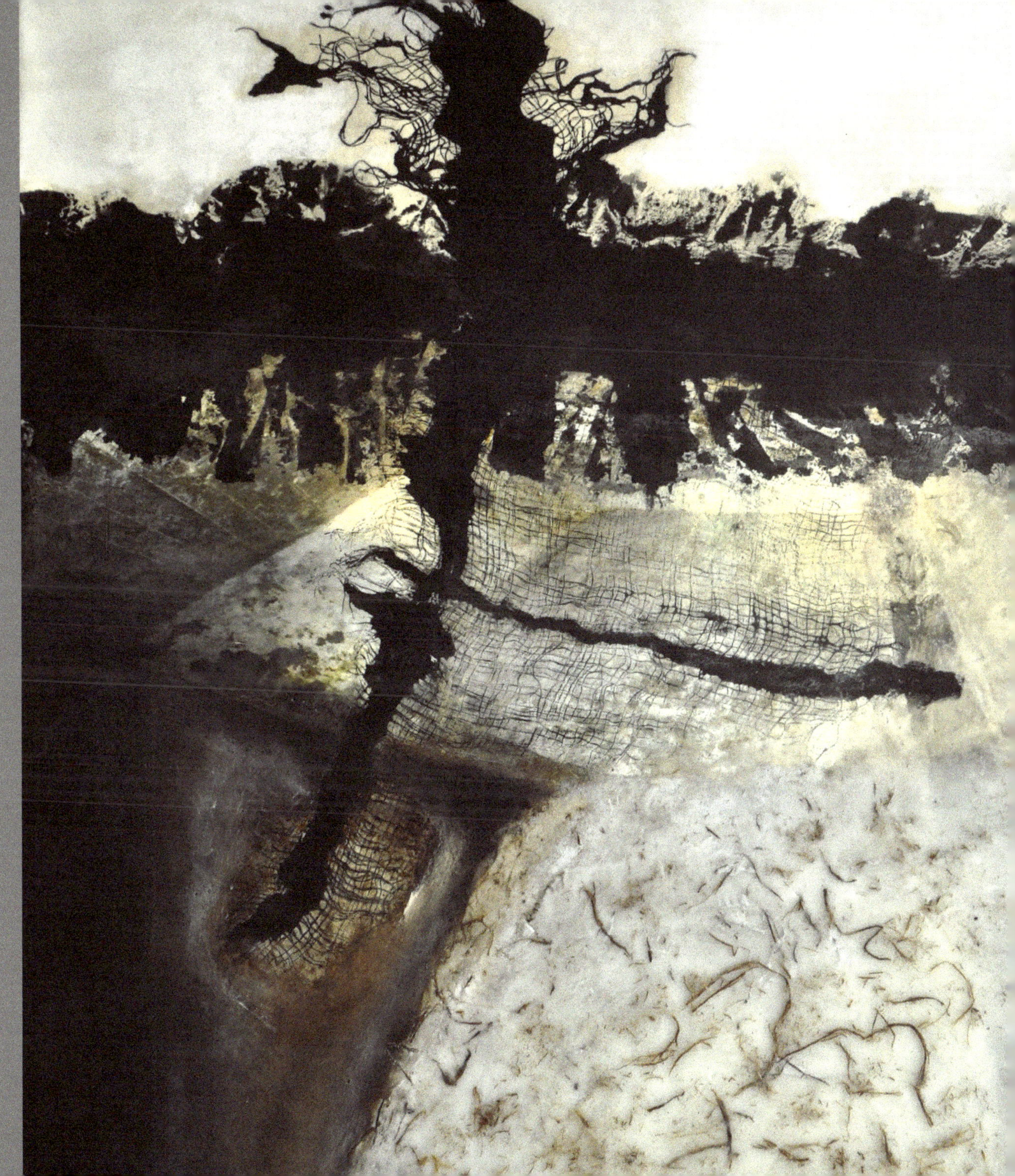

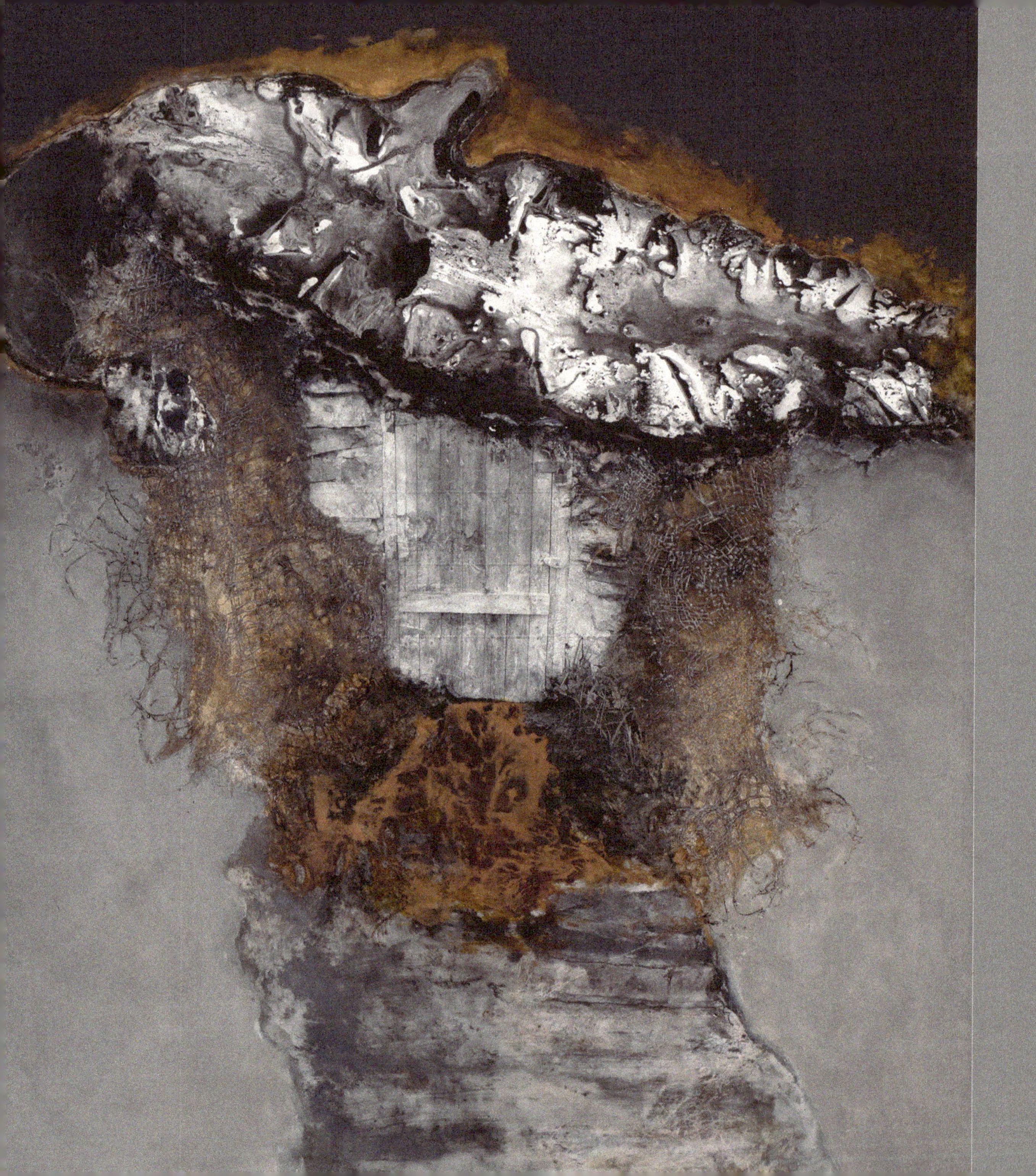

Root Cellar # 31
12″ x 12″ (30.5 x 30.5 cm)
2020

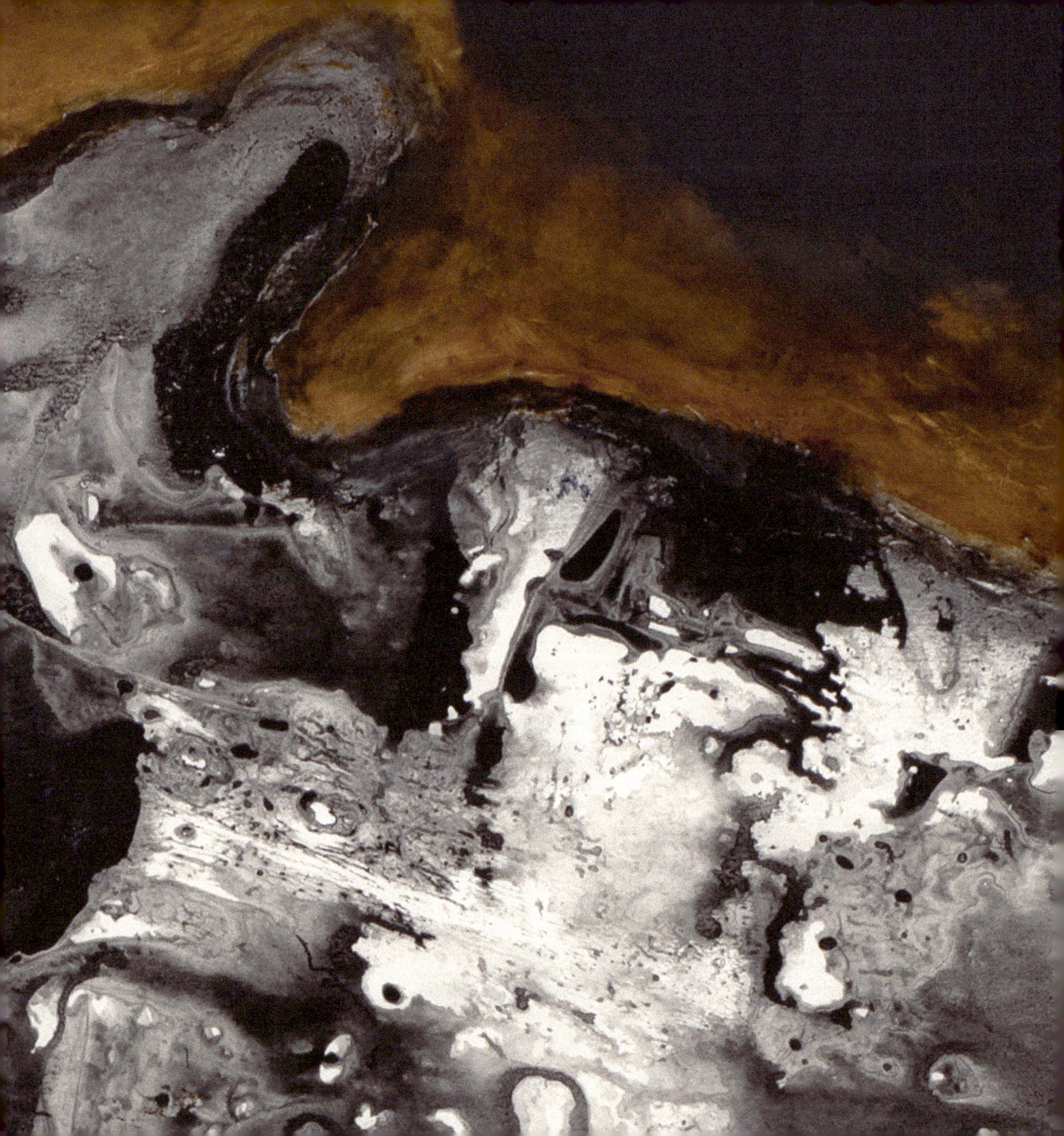

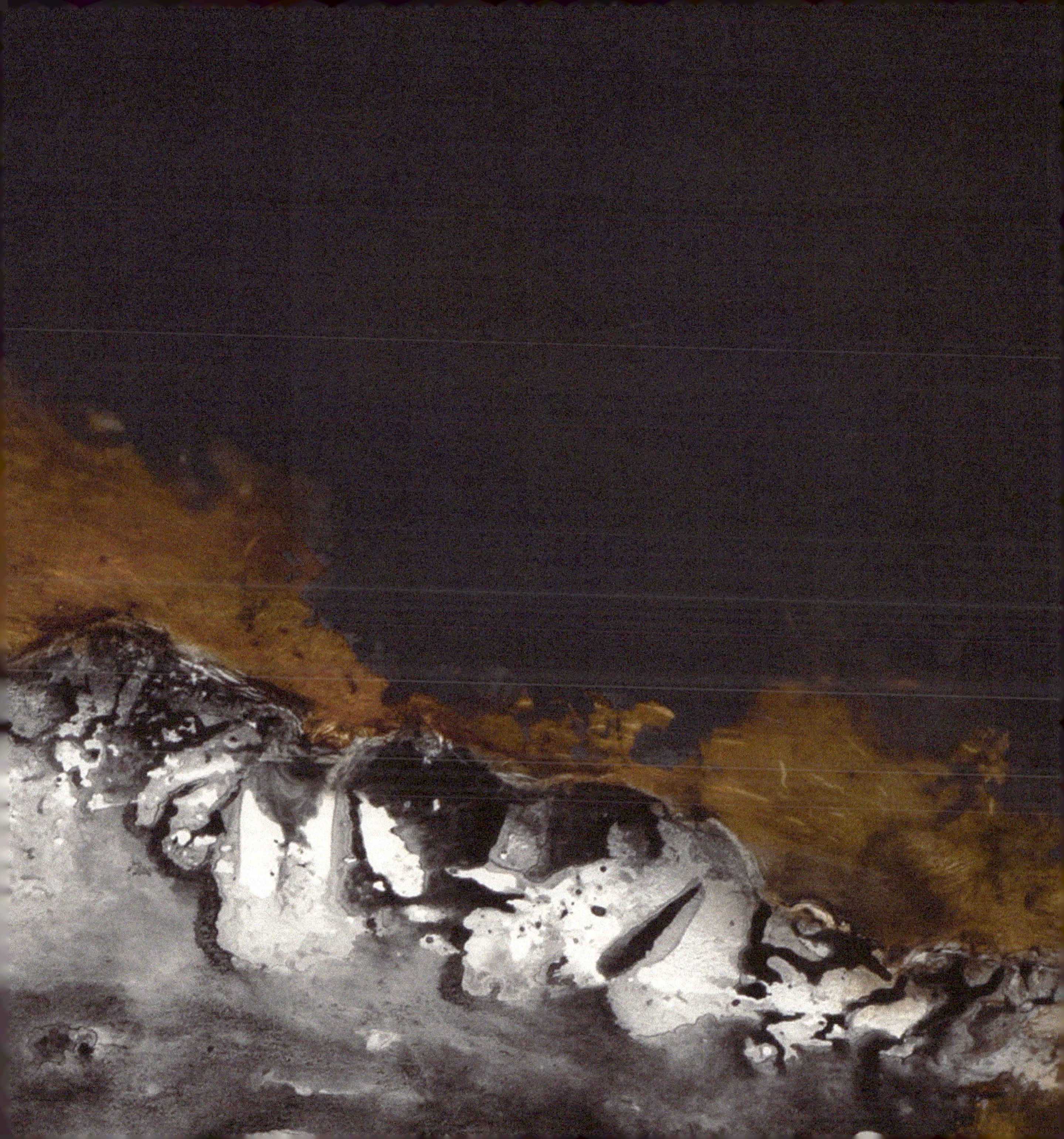

Root Cellar # 13
12" x 12" (30.5 x 30.5 cm)
2017

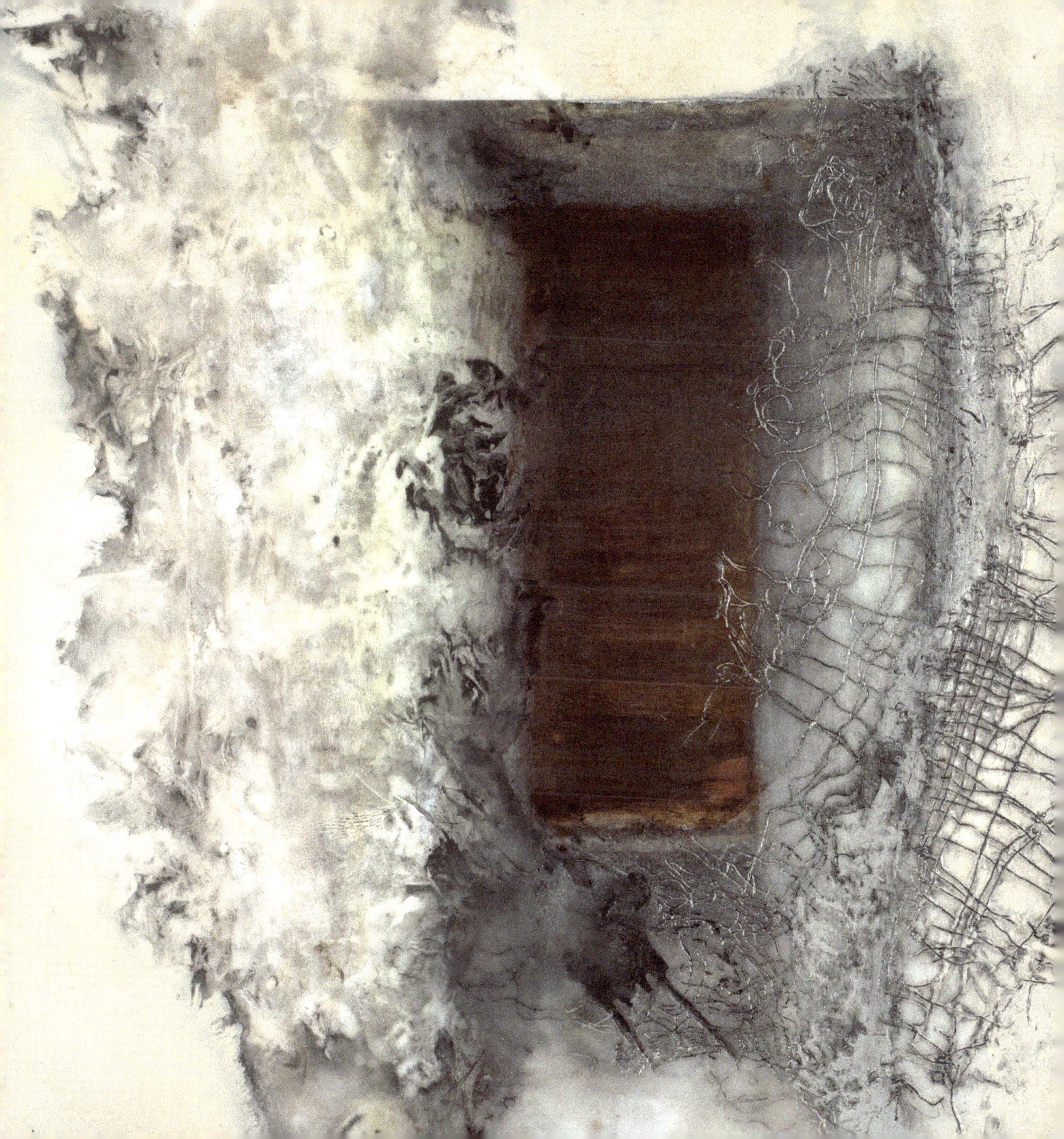

Root Cellar # 8
20" x 24" (50.8 x 61 cm)
2017

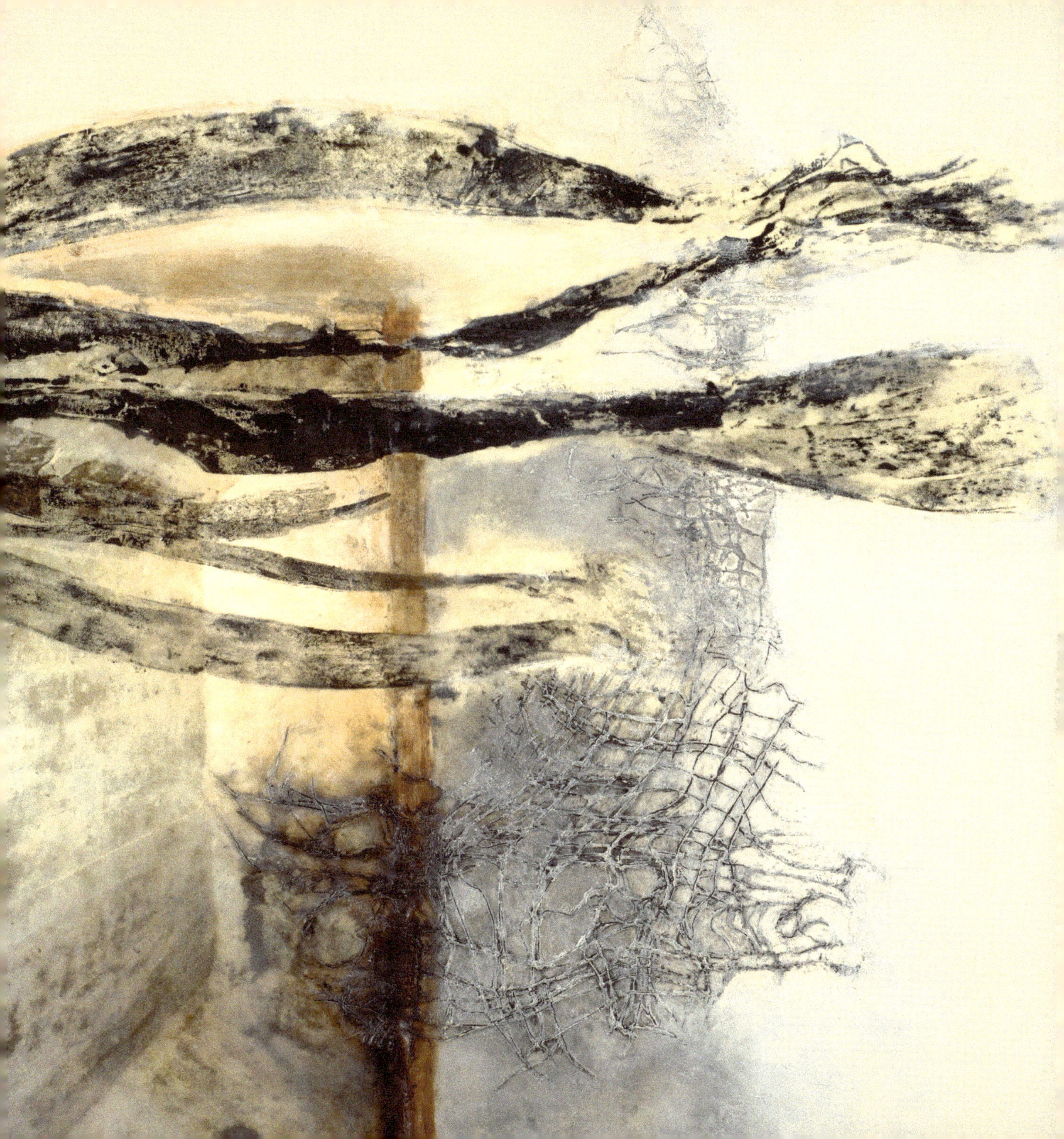

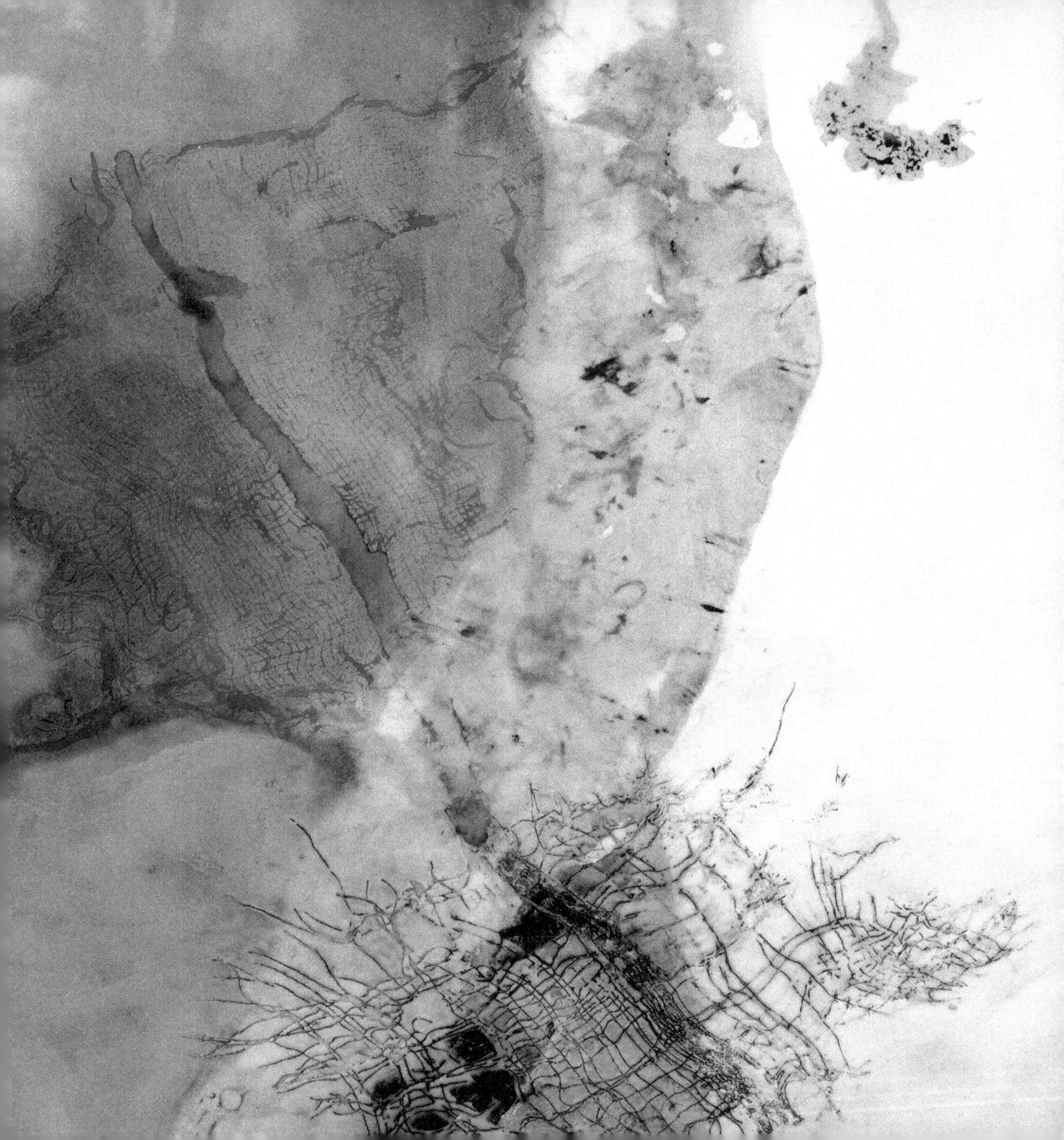

Root Cellar # 3
24" x 20" (61 x 50.8 cm)
2017

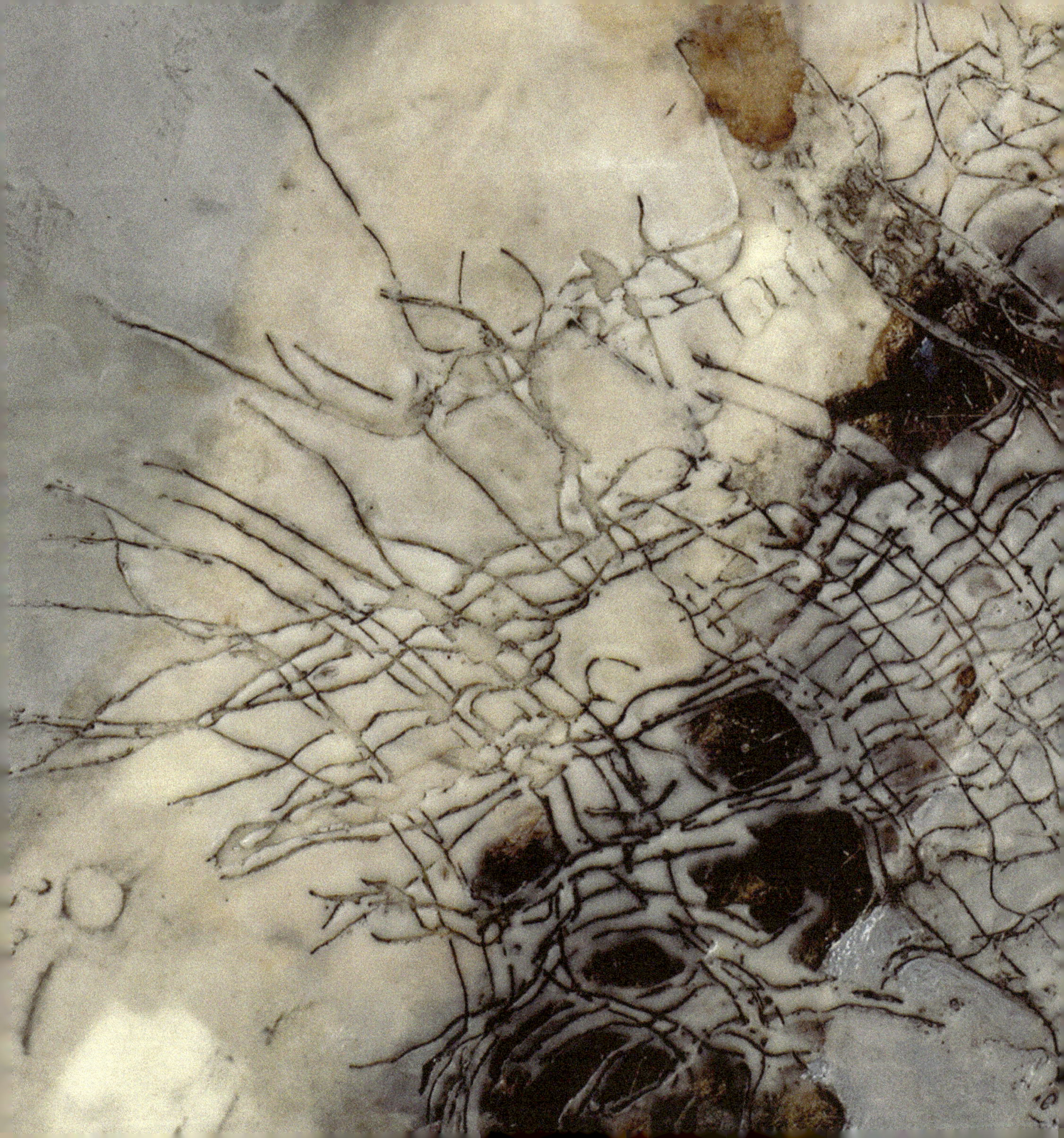

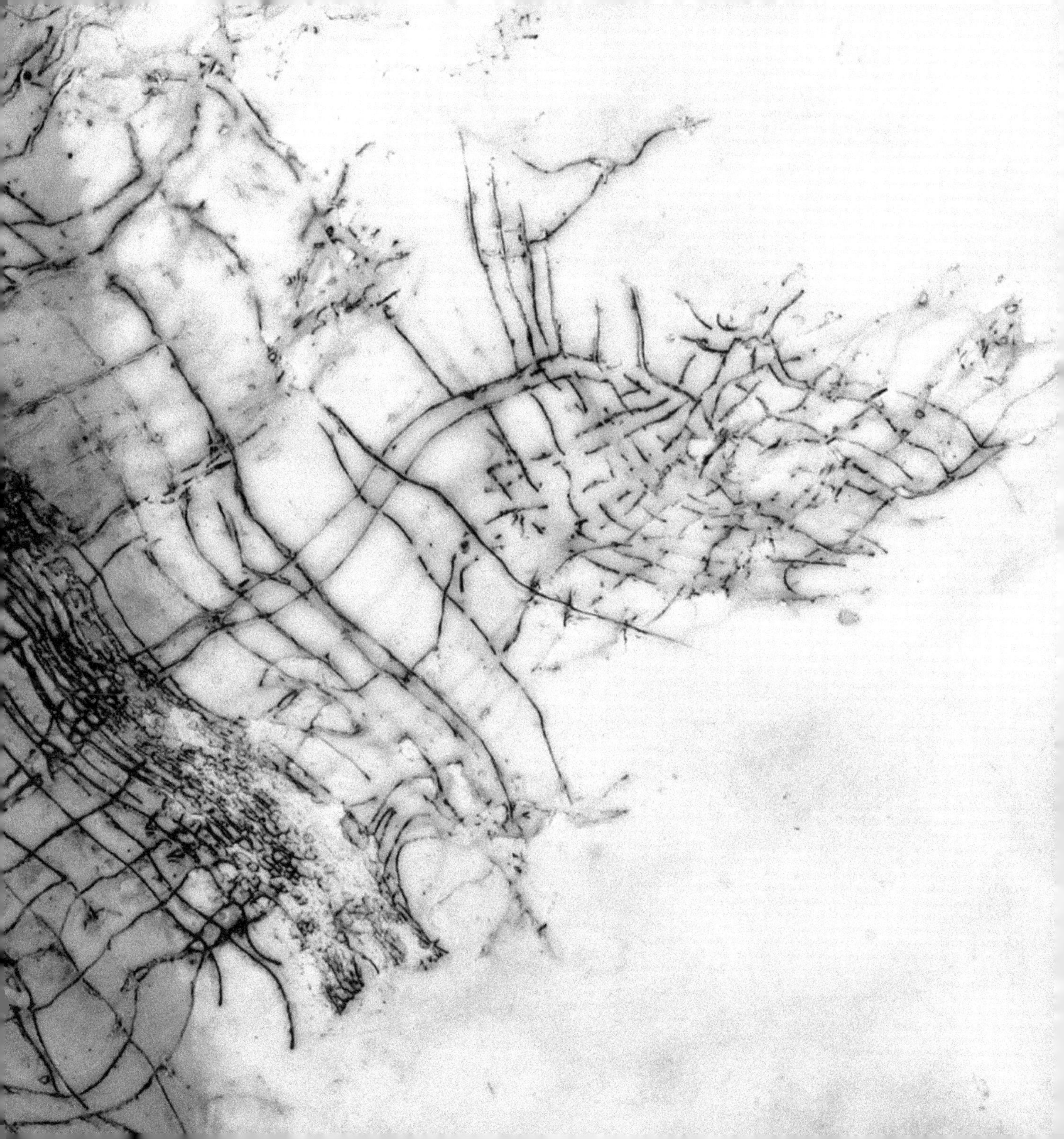

Root Cellar Meditation # 1 (with detail)

24 x 20 inches (61 cm x 50.8 cm)
mixed media: pigment stick, encaustic, Sumi ink sea-weed print on Rives lightweight paper on panel
2017
available from Sivarulrasa Gallery, Almonte, ON

Root Cellar Meditation # 22 (with detail)

12 x 12 inches (30.5 x 30.5 cm)
mixed media: pigment stick, encaustic, Sumi ink sea-weed print on Rives lightweight paper on panel
2018
in private collection

Root Cellar Meditation # 27

24 x 20 inches (61 cm x 50.8 cm)
mixed media: pigment stick, digital transfer, encaustic, Sumi ink seaweed print on Rives lightweight paper on panel
2017
in private collection

Root Cellar Meditation # 29

24 x 20 inches (61 cm x 50.8 cm)
mixed media: pigment stick, digital transfer, encaustic, Sumi ink seaweed print on Rives lightweight paper on panel
2018
available from Christina Parker Gallery, St. John's, NL

Root Cellar Meditation # 4 (with detail)

24 x 20 inches (61 cm x 50.8 cm)
mixed media: pigment stick, encaustic, Sumi ink seaweed print on Rives lightweight paper on panel
2017
available from Sivarulrasa Gallery, Almonte, ON

Root Cellar Meditation # 9

24 x 20 inches (61 cm x 50.8 cm)
mixed media: pigment stick, encaustic, Sumi ink seaweed print on Rives lightweight paper on panel
2017
in private collection

Root Cellar Meditation # 5

24 x 20 inches (61 cm x 50.8 cm)
mixed media: pigment stick, encaustic, Sumi ink seaweed print on Rives lightweight paper on panel
2017
in private collection

Root Cellar Meditation # 6 (with 2 details)

24 x 20 inches (61 cm x 50.8 cm)
mixed media: pigment stick, encaustic, Sumi ink seaweed print on Rives lightweight paper on panel
2017
in private collection

Root Cellar Meditation # 26

24 x 20 inches (61 cm x 50.8 cm)
mixed media: pigment stick, digital transfer, encaustic, Sumi ink seaweed print on Rives lightweight paper on panel
2018
available from Sivarulrasa Gallery, Almonte, ON

Root Cellar Meditation # 10

24 x 20 inches (61 cm x 50.8 cm)
mixed media: pigment stick, encaustic, Sumi ink seaweed print on Rives lightweight paper on panel
2017
available from Christina Parker Gallery, St. John's, NL

Root Cellar Meditation # 7

24 x 20 inches (61 cm x 50.8 cm)
mixed media: pigment stick, encaustic, Sumi ink seaweed print on Rives lightweight paper on panel
2017
contact the artist

Root Cellar Meditation # 11 (with detail)

20 x 17 inches (50.8 cm x 43.2 cm)
mixed media: ink, pigment stick, encaustic, Sumi
ink seaweed print on Kitikata paper on panel
2017
available from Sivarulrasa Gallery, Almonte, ON

Root Cellar Meditation # 18 (with detail)

24 x 20 inches (61 cm x 50.8 cm)
mixed media: pigment stick, digital transfer, encaustic, Sumi ink seaweed print on Rives lightweight paper on panel
2017
in private collection

Root Cellar Meditation # 24

10 x 10 inches (25.4 cm x 25.4 cm)
mixed media: pigment stick, digital transfer, encaustic, Sumi ink seaweed print on Rives lightweight paper on panel
2018
available from Sivarulrasa Gallery, Almonte, ON

Root Cellar Meditation # 23

12 x 12 inches (30.5 cm x 30.5 cm)
mixed media: pigment stick, encaustic, Sumi ink seaweed print on Rives lightweight paper on panel
2017
in private collection

Root Cellar Meditation # 16 (with detail)

24 x 20 inches (61 cm x 50.8 cm)
mixed media: pigment stick, encaustic, Sumi ink seaweed print on Rives lightweight paper on panel
2017
available from Christina Parker Gallery, St. John's, NL

Root Cellar Meditation # 21

33 x 26 inches (83.8 cm x 66 cm)
mixed media: pigment stick, digital transfer, encaustic, Sumi ink seaweed print on Rives lightweight paper on panel
2017
available from Christina Parker Gallery, St. John's, NL

Root Cellar Meditation # 17

26 x 20 inches (66 cm x 50.8 cm)
mixed media: pigment stick, digital transfer, encaustic, Sumi ink seaweed print on Rives lightweight paper on panel
2017
available from Sivarulrasa Gallery, Almonte, ON

Root Cellar Meditation # 31 (with detail)

24 x 20 inches (61 cm x 50.8 cm)
mixed media: pigment stick, encaustic, Sumi ink seaweed print on Rives lightweight paper on panel
2020
available from Sivarulrasa Gallery, Almonte, ON

Root Cellar Meditation # 13

12 x 12 inches (30.5 cm x 30.5 cm)
mixed media: pigment stick, digital trasfer, encaustic, Sumi
ink seaweed print on Rives lightweight paper on panel
2017
in private collection

Root Cellar Meditation # 8

20 x 24 inches (50.8 cm x 61 cm)
mixed media: pigment stick, encaustic, Sumi ink seaweed print on Rives lightweight paper on panel
2017
available from Christina Parker Gallery, St. John's, NL

Root Cellar Meditation # 3 (with detail)

24 x 20 inches (61 cm x 50.8 cm)
mixed media: pigment stick, encaustic, Sumi ink seaweed print on Rives lightweight paper on panel
2017
available from Christina Parker Gallery, St. John's, NL

opposite Emily Deming's essay

Root Cellar Meditation # 14

12 x 12 inches (30.5 cm x 30.5 cm)
mixed media: ink, pigment stick, digital transfer,encaustic, Sumi ink seaweed print on clay-coat paper on panel
2017
available from Christina Parker Gallery, St. John's, NL

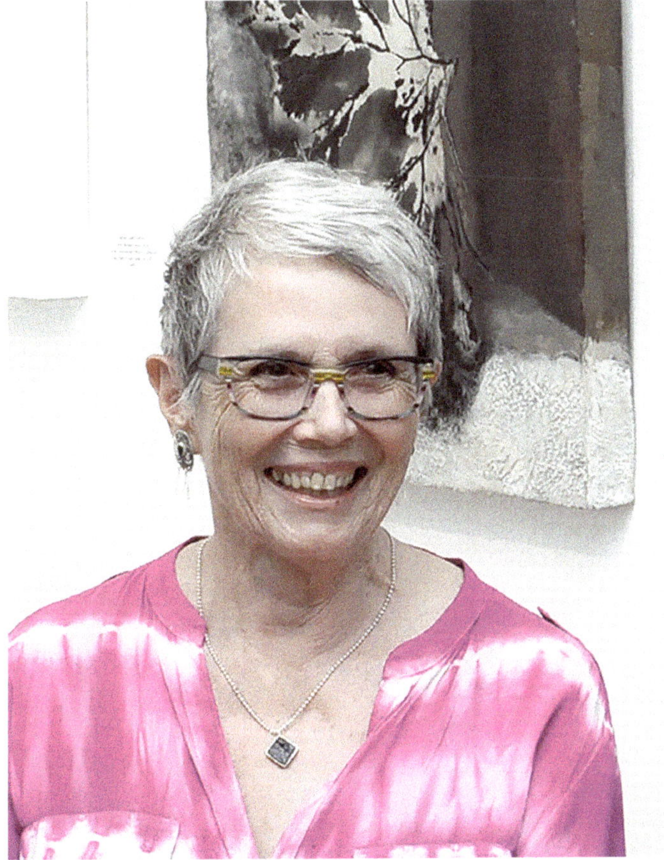

Carol Bajen-Gahm is an artist from Massachusetts with a master's degree in jazz composition. She has created installations combining music and art, but now concentrates on painting at her studio in Torbay, Newfoundland, Canada.

She first came to Newfoundland in 2002 for a painting residency at Pouch Cove and the next year, she and her husband, Rex Passion, affected by the light, landscape, and people, bought a house and studio on the ocean in Torbay, just outside the capital city of St. John's. In 2012 they became permanent residents of Canada.

In 2009 Carol invited R&F Paints of Kingston, New York to come to Newfoundland to do an encaustic workshop. R&F presented two days of printmaking using their pigment sticks at St. Michael's Printshop in St. John's, and a two day encaustic workshop at Carol's studio in Torbay. They left their state-of-the-art equipment at the studio and Carol became an at-large instructor, presenting encaustic and pigment stick workshops.

Between 2003 and 2006 she attended residencies in Costa Rica, Dorland Mountain, California, and Westport Island, Maine. In 2006 she received a Joan Mitchell grant to attend the Santa Fe Institute of Art. She returned to Costa Rica in January of 2016, and later that year, attended the Two Rooms Residency at Duntara, an outport community on the Bonavista peninsula of Newfoundland.

Her abstract oil and encaustic mixed media works explore the effects of place and time on the inner and outer landscape and have been exhibited internationally. Since 2004 she has been represented by the Christina Parker Gallery in St. John's, Newfoundland and since 2018 by Sivarulrasa Gallery in Almonte, Ontario.

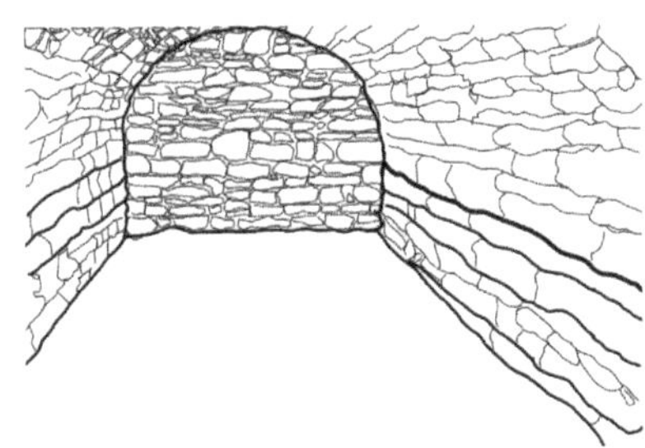

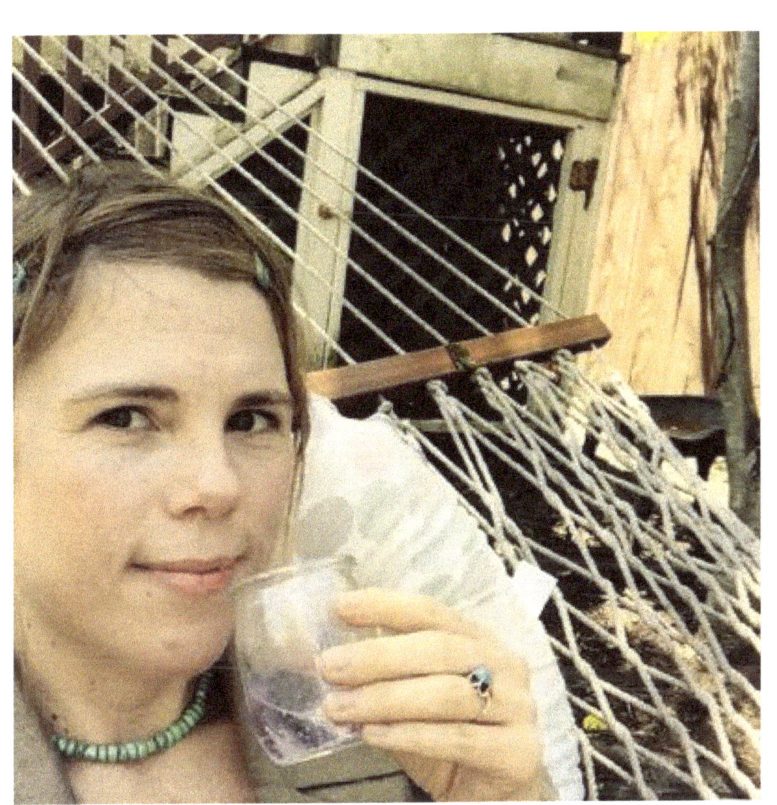

Emily Deming is a freelance writer who came back to writing mid-life after an academic and professional career in earth and planetary sciences and the oil industry. While switching careers, she immigrated, started a family and suffered personal losses. She understands upheaval, does not silo science from art, almost never panics, and finds the most humour in the things she takes the most seriously.

She has written for CBC, Atlantic Business Magazine, The Newfoundland Quarterly, The Scope, East Coast Living, The Overcast and others, about people, food, drink, arts, culture and travel and covered/poked fun at City Hall with her weekly column "Notes from the Rafters" at TheOvercast.ca. Her work covering the Snelgrove Trial in 2017 led to an opportunity to work with Documentarian Chris Brookes from Battery Radio on a GPS based podcast App "Consent: walk the walk," which won international acclaim.

www.ingramcontent.com/pod-product-compliance
Ingram Content Group UK Ltd.
Pitfield, Milton Keynes, MK11 3LW, UK
UKHW061950290726
14090UKWH00021B/1156